LONELY PLANET'S

BEST IN TRAVEL

2022

The best destinations, journeys and experiences for the year ahead

TOP 10 COUNTRIES

1 COOK ISLANDS 14

2 NORWAY 20

3 MAURITIUS 26

4 BELIZE 32

5 SLOVENIA 38

6 ANGUILLA 44

7 OMAN 50

8 NEPAL 56

9 MALAWI 62

10 EGYPT 68

TOP 10 CITIES

1 AUCKLAND, NEW ZEALAND 76

2 TAIPEI, TAIWAN 82

3 FREIBURG, GERMANY 88

4 ATLANTA, USA 94

5 LAGOS, NIGERIA 100

6 NICOSIA/LEFKOSIA, CYPRUS 106

7 DUBLIN, IRELAND 112

8 MÉRIDA, MEXICO 118

9 FLORENCE, ITALY 124

10 GYEONGJU, SOUTH KOREA 130

TOP 10 REGIONS

Top left: beautiful Shoal Bay in Anguilla, an island in the Eastern Caribbean.
Top right: Bulguk-sa temple pavilion in the South Korean city of Gyeongju.

Above: the New River Gorge bridge in a new national park of the same name in West Virginia, USA.

INTRODUCTION

by Tom Hall

Welcome to *Best in Travel 2022*. This year we're a little more excited than usual to bring you our rundown of the top countries, cities and regions to visit in the months ahead. That's because, after an enforced hiatus, it's time to take those long-postponed travel plans off the shelf and make them a reality. We certainly are.

Perhaps looking at the map with pent-up excitement you feel a few suggestions from the experts could be helpful. That's where *Best in Travel* comes in. The lists in this book celebrate the world in all its wonderful, enticing variety, from the lagoons and forests of the Cook Islands to the waterfalls and mountains of Iceland's Westfjords, via Auckland's natural and urban delights. There are new takes on popular destinations including Norway and Burgundy, and visits

to Florence, Mérida, Puerto Rico, Shikoku and more along the way.

But as we reach 2022, we must first reflect on the extraordinary two years that have changed not just travel but our whole lives.

By March 2020 I had already visited Greece and Nashville and taken a train from Budapest to Amsterdam. That journey finished with the anticipation of plenty more

Dynjandi waterfall in Iceland's Westfjords: wild places and natural wonders will be sought after in 2022.

to come, with little attention being paid to stories of a new virus causing all kinds of concern in China. Within a few short weeks though, my and everyone else's travel plans – along with so much else in our lives – were brought to the hardest of abrupt halts. Few of us could ever have imagined that the ceaseless waves of international movement that had become a constant part of the

THE BEST IN TRAVEL PROMISE

WHERE IS THE BEST PLACE TO VISIT RIGHT NOW?

This is the most hotly contested topic at Lonely Planet. As self-confessed travel geeks, our global community of staff and writers roams widely most years, exploring almost every destination on the planet in the process.

Where is the best place to visit right now? We ask everyone at Lonely Planet, from our writers and editors all the way to our online family of social media influencers. And each year they come up with hundreds of places that are special right now, offer new things for travellers to see or do, or are overlooked and underrated.

Amid fierce debate, the list is whittled down by our panel of travel experts to just 10 countries, 10 regions and 10 cities. Each is chosen for its topicality, unique experiences and 'wow' factor. We also take sustainable travel seriously – helping you to have a positive impact wherever you choose to go.

Put simply, what remains in the pages that follow is the cream of this year's travel picks, courtesy of Lonely Planet: 10 countries, 10 regions and 10 cities to inspire you to explore for yourself.

So what are you waiting for?

© ENZOJZ | GETTY IMAGES

everyday could be stopped at all, let alone so quickly. We saw and experienced incredible scrambles to get home, or tough decisions to stay put. And with this sudden lockdown, airports became ghost towns, borders closed, sights were shuttered.

Those months of compulsory hibernation provided time to reflect. 2021 demonstrated just how much travelling, and the freedom to travel, is a core part of life for so many of us. We soon learned how much we miss it when it's gone. Those planes and trains and boats that take us on trips connect us with each other and the world in more meaningful ways than a thousand Zoom calls ever can. The pandemic has separated families, postponed celebrations and put journeys of a lifetime on hold. The impact went beyond individuals. Thousands of jobs in tourism and related spheres like transport, conservation and education have been lost or imperilled.

The Covid-19 pandemic has been unprecedentedly disruptive, but has also pushed emerging concerns about travel to the fore. Carbon emissions from aviation have dropped to levels close to targets for avoiding catastrophic global warming. Fragile and precious

> ## "When it comes to responsible tourism, *Best in Travel* emphasises ideas you can act on, wherever you're going."

places have had an unexpected but very welcome moment of respite. Communities around the globe have experienced their cities, parks, villages and islands without crowds of visitors, floods of flights and daily disruption. New and diverse voices have had a chance to speak about travel and their experiences of it, challenging old models for publishers like Lonely Planet. These developments feel like one-way streets that will change travel forever once it rebounds.

And rebounding it certainly is. All the signs are that as soon as it is safe to do so, countries will welcome visitors again, albeit tentatively. The arguments in favour of mass travel and tourism remain undeniable, with benefits for both society at large and the individual in particular. Lonely Planet has always been a champion of travel as a force for good, and we're determined to be there for travellers again when they're ready, and the time is right, to set off on the next adventure.

This sense of a recovery has encouraged many of us to think about 'new travel resolutions', how to explore our planet more responsibly in the future, considering low-impact ways both to get to a destination and then to engage with it once there. *Best in Travel 2021* highlighted change-makers in the areas of community,

sustainability and diversity to help make informed choices easier. We've continued that focus in this year's selection and are delighted to be working with many contributors for the first time, contributors who are experts on the places they've written about for us. When it comes to responsible tourism, *Best in Travel* emphasises ideas you can act on wherever you're going.

This return to exploring the world is going to be tentative and fragmented. Slowly but surely though, 2022 will be the year when dreams should become reality again. Whether you're simply in need of a weekend city break or are longing for that special trip you promised yourself on an especially bad day during lockdown, what a golden year this could be. With countries still gearing up for a resumption of tourism, this just might be one of the best times to take the chance to see Egypt's pyramids, trek the Himalaya in Nepal or dive headlong into Taipei's cityscape. It will take a while for visitor numbers to creep up, but, when they do, in many cases it will be against a backdrop of different, but equally appealing and often forward-looking experiences in destinations, coming together to renew everyone's love of the best in travel.

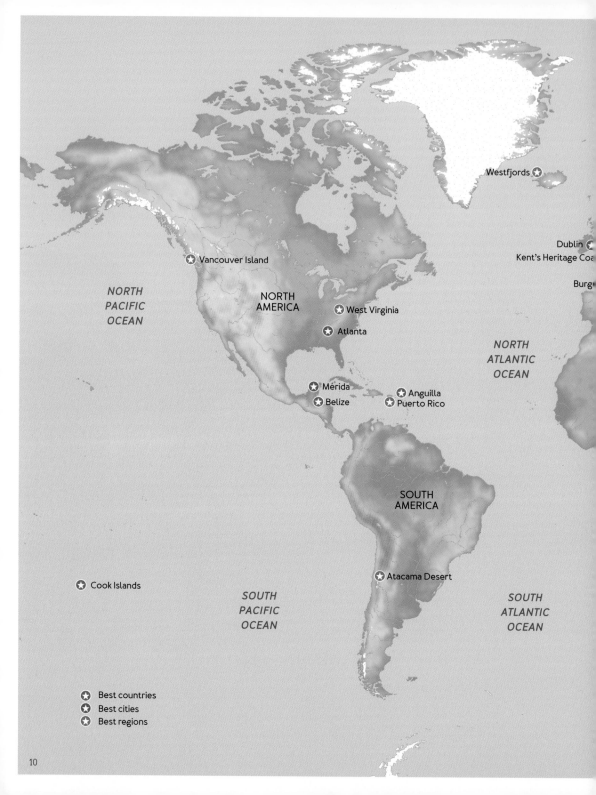

Westfjords ✪

Dublin ✪
Kent's Heritage Coa

Burg✪

NORTH
PACIFIC
OCEAN

✪ Vancouver Island

NORTH
AMERICA

✪ West Virginia

✪ Atlanta

NORTH
ATLANTIC
OCEAN

✪ Mérida
✪ Belize

✪ Anguilla
✪ Puerto Rico

SOUTH
AMERICA

✪ Cook Islands

✪ Atacama Desert

SOUTH
PACIFIC
OCEAN

SOUTH
ATLANTIC
OCEAN

✪ Best countries
✪ Best cities
✪ Best regions

10

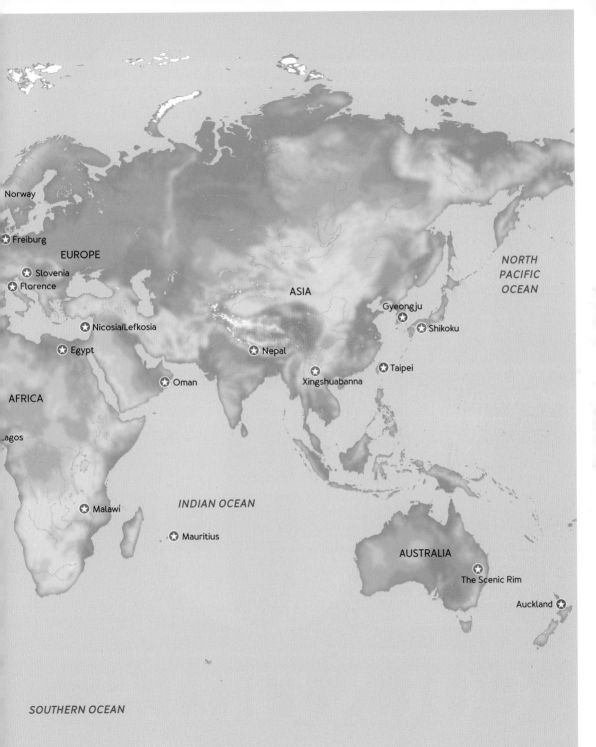

Norway

⭐ Freiburg

EUROPE

⭐ Slovenia
⭐ Florence

⭐ Nicosia/Lefkosia

⭐ Egypt

AFRICA

Lagos

⭐ Malawi

⭐ Mauritius

INDIAN OCEAN

ASIA

Gyeongju
⭐
⭐ Shikoku

⭐ Nepal

⭐ Oman

⭐ Xingshuabanna

⭐ Taipei

NORTH
PACIFIC
OCEAN

AUSTRALIA

⭐ The Scenic Rim

Auckland ⭐

SOUTHERN OCEAN

TOP
10
COUNTRIES

COOK ISLANDS

GOOD TO KNOW

UTC -10hr

Cook Islands dollar

Cook Islands Māori, English.

Air New Zealand has direct flights linking Auckland to Rarotonga.

• www.cookislands. travel
• www.cookislands news.com
• *Patterns of the Past: Tattoo Revival in the Cook Islands* Therese Mangos & John Utanga

Authentic Polynesian traditions and a bold and pioneering approach to the challenges facing South Pacific nations combine in the proudly independent Cook Islands. Diverse landscapes framed by the remote expanses of the world's biggest ocean promise active adventure, cultural interaction and culinary delights. When international travel recovers from Covid-19, innovative strategies focused on sustainability are set to ensure the Cooks emerge as an intriguing and surprising destination.

REMOTE IN THE SOUTH PACIFIC
Welcome to one of the planet's most isolated, spread-out countries – 15 volcano-formed islands comprising just 240 sq km, dotted across two million sq km of Polynesia. Rarotonga is the chain's largest and most populous island, and also its most cosmopolitan. Here, especially in the laidback capital Avarua, Cook Islands traditions blend comfortably with cafe culture and an emerging artisan and organic food scene. The islands of Aitutaki and 'Atiu offer contrasting reasons to visit – Aitutaki curls around one of the South Pacific's most stunning lagoons, while forested 'Atiu is a rocky, reef-fringed outcrop speckled with limestone caves. Far from the main island, sleepy Mitiaro, Ma'uke and Mangaia all showcase Polynesian culture. And even farther from Raro, more than 1000km in fact, sparsely populated atolls make up the rest of the nation, including Manihiki, where life revolves around pearl farming.

A ROADMAP TO SUSTAINABILITY
For several years the Cook Islands have been taking significant steps to develop and support a sustainable tourism industry. Created in mid-2017, Marae Moana (translating to 'Sacred Ocean') is a multiple-use marine park covering the country's entire exclusive economic zone – over 1,976,000 sq km – and is the planet's largest protected area. The legislation creates specific marine sanctuaries, extending to 93km around each of the Cooks' 15 islands, in which all commercial fishing or seabed resource mining is prohibited. Fishing or resource exploration in the rest of the marine park can only be done on a sustainable basis.

Also looking to the future is the Cook Islands' ongoing Fossil Free initiative. Thirteen of the nation's islands are now completely free of diesel generators, and renewable solar energy is increasingly widespread across the country.

As part of the Te Kaveinga Nui

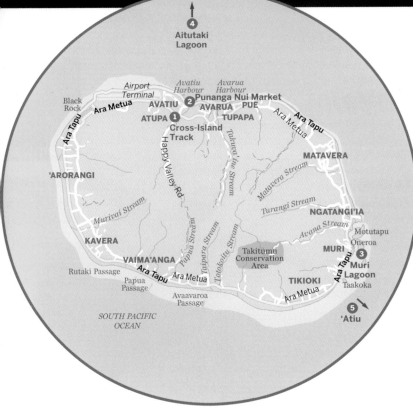

HIGHLIGHTS

1 **Cross-Island Track** Hike coast to coast across the rugged, forested interior of Rarotonga.

2 **Punanga Nui Market** Island flavours and music at Saturday morning's biggest attraction.

3 **Muri Lagoon** Snorkelling, paddleboarding and relaxing amid Rarotonga's sheltered waters.

4 **Aitutaki Lagoon** Discover your own deserted *motu* (island) by kayak.

5 **'Atiu** Combine caving and birdwatching on this remote island.

> **" The Cook Islands are the ultimate tropical escape destination with a beautiful environment, welcoming people and a growing environmental ethos across the tourism and hospitality industry."**

CORRINA TUCKER
STORYTELLERS ECO CYCLE AND WALKING TOURS

National Sustainable Development Plan, the government is striving to balance environmental impacts with the country's reliance on tourists (around 70% of the Cook Islands' GDP is generated by tourism), and in recent years local operators have been strongly encouraged to make sustainable choices and develop eco-aware business strategies. Key to this transition is the Mana Tiaki Eco Certification programme, which ensures local travel industry providers adhere to conservation-focused best practices. Mana Tiaki-certified tourism operators include Rarotonga's Storytellers Eco Cycle and Walking Tours – environmental issues are regularly highlighted on their experiences, and they also fundraise and donate a percentage of profits to local NGOs and community initiatives aimed at sustainable development. Also certified are Tik-e Tours, who offer zero-emission transport and travel services around Rarotonga on e-bikes and in electric tuk tuks. Beyond their luxury safari-style tents and emphasis on green practices and solar energy, Ikurangi Eco Retreats earned their certificate by supporting island projects like Te Are Manu,

Rarotonga's charity-funded and volunteer-run vet clinic.

COOK ISLANDS CULTURE

To discover Cook Islands culture and try local cuisine, a visit to Rarotonga's Saturday morning Punanga Nui Market is essential. Dishes to try include smoked marlin and *rukau* (steamed taro leaves), and local cultural groups performing Cook Islands' music and dance are a weekly attraction. Ngametua Mamanu from Tumutoa Tours is also a market regular who, along with his wife Mania, offers activities for travellers to Rarotonga including feasts cooked in a traditional *umu kai* (earth oven).

WHEN TO GO

MAR & APR
The end of the cyclone season (usually Nov-Mar) brings clear, sunny days.

JUL & AUG
The year's lowest rainfall means walking trails are drier. The week-long Te Maeva Nui Festival celebrates independence.

SEP & OCT
Warmer weather and reduced humidity make this a good time for active travellers to visit.

Visitors are encouraged to help prepare the authentic Polynesian meal and weave serving platters from local plants.

For travellers keen to contribute directly to the local community, opportunities include supporting the environmental work of the Te Ipukarea Society. Past initiatives have included the eradication of feral rats on remote atolls, supporting endangered endemic birds and setting up Rarotonga's first recycling centre. Donations are also welcomed by the Te Are Manu vet clinic, where the animal welfare work they undertake means Rarotonga's stray dog population is much lower than on other Pacific islands. And at the Discover Marine and Wildlife Eco Centre there's a strong focus on supporting ocean environments, and admission fees help support a bird and sea turtle rescue facility.

In one of the world's smallest countries in the middle of the planet's largest ocean, it's easy to join the locals in making a big difference.

Above: ancient rainforest on 'Atiu island harbours a wealth of bird and animal life – and some terrifically twisty trees.

Left: a donation to Rarotonga's Discover Marine and Wildlife Eco Centre helps to support and rescue endangered green turtles.

Previous spread: Rarotonga with its airstrip on the left.

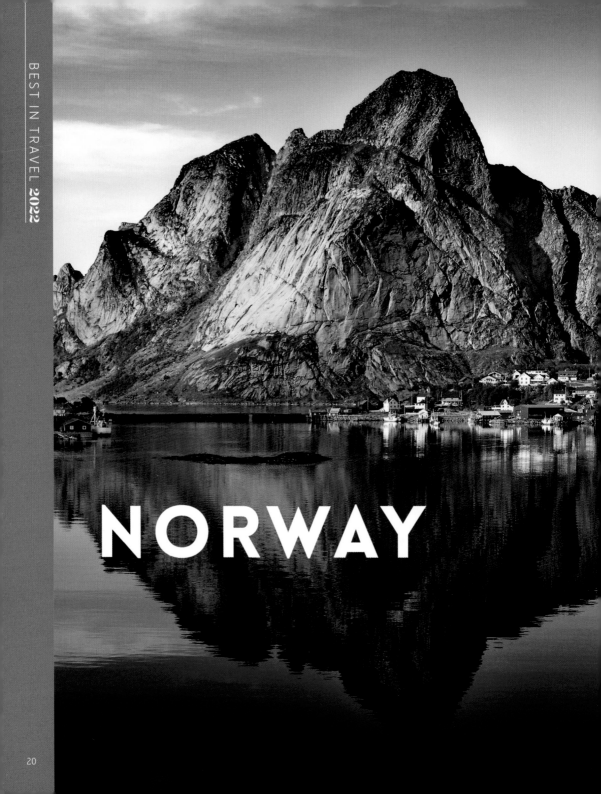

NORWAY

© PREVIOUS PAGE: MATT MUNRO | LONELY PLANET; ABOVE: JUSTIN FOULKES | LONELY PLANET

GOOD TO KNOW

UTC +2hr

Norwegian krone

Norwegian, English.

Frequent flights to Oslo from European cities, plus fast train connections to neighbouring capitals, including Stockholm and Copenhagen.

• *The Nordic Theory of Everything: In Search of a Better Life* Anu Partanen
• *The Almost Nearly Perfect People* Michael Booth
• *A Death in the Family* Karl Ove Knausgaard

Where's the best place to live on Earth? According to the Human Development Index, it's Norway (it's actually taken top spot several years running). With inspiring landscapes, epic wilderness and world-beating fjords, Norway is almost unfairly blessed in terms of natural beauty. And it's also leading the charge on sustainability, green tech and cultural highlights – the brand new Munch Museum and refurbished National Museum will enjoy their first full seasons of being open in 2022.

IMPROVING ON PERFECTION
Somehow, this Nordic powerhouse seems to excel at everything it does. Whether it's education, healthcare, equality, income or just plain old quality of life, Norway has an uncanny knack for doing things right.

But there's still room for improvement. The bills for those widely-envied stats on wealth, welfare and well-being have largely been paid for by the country being one of the world's leading oil and gas-extracting nations, industries that still account for 17% of the national economy.

Things are shifting, though. Conscious of climate change, Norway is cleaning up its act. Renewable energy is ramping up fast – 99% of electricity now comes from hydropower, and the government has committed to carbon neutrality by 2030. It's a world leader in green transport, too, with one of the world's highest quotas of electric cars per capita – already, 58% of new cars in Norway are electric, and by 2025, petrol and diesel car sales will be banned outright.

Norway's ferries are also going electric. The world's first 100% electric vessel, *Future of the Fjords*, began operating in 2018, recently joined by a sister ship, *Legacy of the Fjords*. Electric ferries are cruising around Oslo and Trondheim, and the Norwegian Public Roads Administration plans to electrify all its vessels by 2030. Even the iconic Hurtigruten, a vital coastal transport link since 1893, is getting on board: the company recently commissioned the world's first hybrid ships, which use battery power to reduce carbon emissions by more than 20%.

SETTING SUSTAINABLE STANDARDS
Sustainable tourism is high on the agenda in Norway. Overtourism has long blighted popular areas such as Unesco-listed Geirangerfjord, photogenic Preikestolen and the spiky summits of the Lofoten Islands. The ancient law of *allemannsretten*

Geirangerfjord and the Seven Sisters waterfalls.

HIGHLIGHTS

1 **Oslo** Art, architecture, history, nature – whatever your interest, Norway's dynamic capital has you covered.

2 **Bergensbanen** Take the country's most spectacular train trip over the snow-strewn Hardangervidda plateau.

3 **Tromsø** Spot the Northern Lights or go dog-sledding from this little polar town inside the Arctic Circle.

4 **Trollstigen** Tackle hairpin curves and spot waterfalls on a corkscrew, sky-scraping road.

5 **Glacier walking** Hike out onto one of Norway's mighty, ancient glaciers.

Ålesund in Norway's far north, known for its Jugendstil (art nouveau) architecture and mighty cod-fishing fleet.

(freedom to roam) permits anyone to explore the countryside without seeking permission, and is a sacred right to many Norwegians – but in an age of mass tourism and social media, it's causing headaches.

To address the issue, authorities have implemented their own Sustainable Destination Standard, awarded to areas that pledge to support the environment, community, cultural heritage and a more sustainable economy. From Lillehammer to Lysefjord, Tromsø to Trysil, there are 14 destinations on the list with 13 more in the pipeline, including scenic Sognefjord, adrenaline capital Voss and Bodø, gateway to the Lofotens.

In many ways, Norwegians are simply relearning old lessons. For centuries, the indigenous Sami have practised their nomadic lifestyle in the far north, living from the land with barely any carbon footprint. Staying with the Sami and experiencing their low-impact way of life ranks as Norway's premier ecotourism option – sleeping in a traditional *lavvu* tent, practising handicrafts and learning ancient recipes for reindeer stew offer not just an insight into the past, but salutary lessons for a more sustainable future. With a bit of luck, you'll spot the Northern Lights, too.

BUILDING GREEN

Norway's architecture is also going green. The FutureBuilt initiative demonstrates how urban development can be achieved in climate-neutral, eco-conscious ways. It's run by six municipalities around Oslo and currently has 56 pilot schemes, ranging from schools to office buildings, providing a blueprint for the rest of Norway to follow.

Several high-profile building projects have been influenced by the initiative, including the long-awaited Munch Museum, dedicated to the painter of *The Scream*; and the redevelopment of the National-museet, Norway's foremost history museum. Opened in late 2021, both are planning big post-Coronavirus programmes for 2022.

Then there's Svart, a circular orb at the base of the Svartisen Glacier that looks like a space-station fallen to Earth and is the world's first energy-positive hotel. Using solar power to offset its construction and energy use, it aims to be self-sufficient in electricity, water and waste management within five years.

And on the Arctic island of Andøya, another futuristic building surfaces in 2023. The Whale, a striking structure resembling the flukes of a whale's tail, will be a centre for cetacean research, and the museum will surely become one of northern Norway's unmissable architectural attractions. Who knows, it might even act as a clarion call for the country to add ending the whaling industry to its long list of achievements.

> **WHEN TO GO**
>
> **MID-JUN TO MID-AUG**
> Plenty of sunshine, moderate temperatures and long days (really long in the north, where the sun doesn't set).
>
> **MAY TO MID-JUN, MID-AUG TO SEP**
> Fewer visitors and generally mild temperatures. Spring growth and autumn colours are highlights.
>
> **OCT-APR**
> Lots of snow and short days, but the best time to see the Northern Lights.

"**Norwegians have a unique affinity with the landscape around them – and you can clearly see that love at work in their architecture.**"

TODD SAUNDERS
ARCHITECT, WWW.SAUNDERS.NO

03

MAURITIUS

GOOD TO KNOW

UTC +4hr

Rupee

French, English, Creole.

Numerous airlines fly into Mauritius' Sir Seewoosagur Ramgoolam International Airport in the island's southeast corner.

• *Mauritius, Réunion & Seychelles* Lonely Planet
• www.tourism-mauritius.mu
• www.mauritian-wildlife.org

Isolation has always been easy in Mauritius, a gloriously beautiful island out in the Indian Ocean. Fringed with coral reefs and transparent waters set against the backdrop of a rugged interior, Mauritius combines a fascinating cultural mix with an intriguing natural setting – not for nothing did Mark Twain compare it with paradise. And at a time when being a long way from anywhere has become more appealing than ever, Mauritius is perfectly placed for a deliciously remote escape.

READY FOR THE REBOUND

Whatever form travel takes in the future, Mauritius is ready. This is a country that has built its reputation among travellers on a rock-solid foundation of exceptional natural beauty, outstanding tourism infrastructure and a commitment to low-impact travel.

When the world stopped travelling in 2020 and 2021, Mauritius took a hit like so many other visitor-dependent economies. Aside from a few scares, it was able to keep the virus at bay: case numbers were low and, were it not for the absence of international tourists, life closely resembled the country's pre-pandemic existence.

All of which means that with the foundations of its tourism industry dormant but otherwise unchanged, and with secure borders and world-class accommodation, Mauritius is ideally placed for our return.

BACK FROM THE BRINK

At the core of what Mauritius can offer is a connection with nature. Diving and snorkelling are possible all around the coastline – face-to-face encounters with fabulous marine life are standard. Off the west coast, whales and dolphins swim close to shore; and the trails of Black River Gorges National Park echo with birdlife and the chittering of macaque monkeys. But it wasn't always like this.

Before the first settlers arrived in Mauritius late in the 16th century, this was a paradise for many other animals, too. When the settlers wiped out the dodo within a generation, Mauritius seemed destined to become a byword for extinction. How times have changed.

The country is now better known for having saved more bird species from the brink of extinction than any other place on Earth. In Black River Gorges, idyllic Vallée de Ferney and the Noah's-Ark-like Île aux Aigrettes,

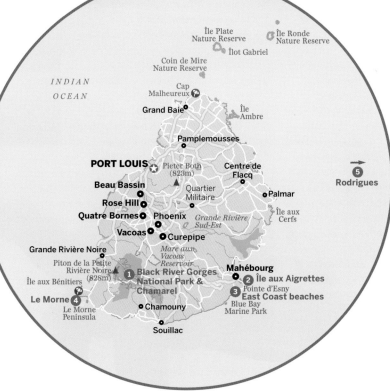

HIGHLIGHTS

1 **Black River Gorges National Park & Chamarel** Explore forests, gorges and waterfalls, then relax in the rum capital of Mauritius.

2 **Île aux Aigrettes** Step back in time with endangered species on this beautiful island.

3 **East Coast beaches** The quiet and spectacular shores Mauritius is famous for.

4 **Le Morne** Climb the island's most dramatic mountain for fantastic views.

5 **Rodrigues** Gloriously remote Mauritian island far from the world and its noise.

> **"Mauritius and Rodrigues are among the rare places on earth where the tide has been turned for many species, and for key habitats. Many of our most beautiful places now offer ecotours for visitors."**
>
> DR VIKASH TATAYAH
> CONSERVATION DIRECTOR, MAURITIAN WILDLIFE FOUNDATION

the pink pigeon, echo parakeet and Mauritian kestrel all fly free and in ever-growing numbers – hugely positive news given that all of these species were down to single figures not so long ago. Also on Île aux Aigrettes and the outlying island of Rodrigues, giant Aldabra tortoises add to the country's quietly burgeoning reputation as the Galapagos of the Indian Ocean.

Even in the face of tragedy, Mauritius has shown that sustainability is deeply rooted in the lives of its people and its tourism industry. When a large tanker ran aground off the island's southeast shore in August 2020, the local people worked tirelessly to clean up the coast and save untold numbers of marine species. And when excursions to swim with dolphins off Flic en Flac along the west coast became too popular for the dolphins' own good, Dolswim emerged as an ecologically responsible operator that is changing the way the entire industry operates. Such initiatives

are aspirations in many countries. In Mauritius, this is just the way they roll.

OPEN TO ALL
Tolerance is a quintessential Mauritian character trait, which is just as well considering how richly diverse the country is. In addition to the countless nationalities who visit, Mauritius is home to a long-established and cohesive population that includes people of Indian, Chinese, French, Creole (African) and South African origin. Perhaps it's because passions rarely run high in this languidly tropical land of plenty. Or maybe it comes from the fact that this is a wonderfully compact island where everyone

WHEN TO GO

DEC-FEB
High season is good for Mauritius' many water activities, though it can be extremely humid and cyclones are possible in January and February.

MAR & APR, OCT & NOV
Warm temperatures, fewer cyclones and good underwater visibility make this a great time to visit.

MAY-SEP
Generally cooler but you're still in the tropics so humidity remains high.

seems to know everybody else. Whatever the reason, tension and intolerance are almost unheard of.

Mauritius is also streets ahead of many countries in the region when it comes to women's rights, although, as everywhere, much remains to be done. Female literacy is above 90%, laws prohibit discrimination on the basis of gender, and younger generations of Mauritians are pushing the country towards a more inclusive future – statistics show that more women in Mauritius are pursuing careers outside

the home, and that intermarriage between ethnic communities is rising.

Visitors to Mauritius have always been treated as warmly welcomed guests. It has also long been one of the safest destinations in the Indian Ocean region. In more recent times, however, Mauritius has evolved to become an inclusive destination that welcomes travellers regardless of their background. All in all, this liberal philosophy brings a whole new meaning to Mauritius' renowned all-inclusive holidays.

Above: make desert-island dreams a reality at Le Morne Brabant.

Left: sheltering under carapaces of up to 120cm long, the giant Aldabra tortoises of Rodrigues and Île aux Aigrettes are a conservation success story.

Previous page: Chamarel Falls.

BELIZE

04

GOOD TO KNOW

UTC -6hr

Belizean Dollar (BZD)

English is the official language; Spanish and English-based Kriol are widely spoken. Several Maya languages are still in active use, as is Garifuna.

Belize's only international airport is Philip SW Goldson, with flights to other airports in the country.

• *The Last Flight of the Scarlet Macaw* Bruce Barcott
• www.sanpedro scoop.com
• www.belizing.com

Nestled between the glittering Caribbean Sea and the rest of Central America is English-speaking Belize, where island vibes and jungle adventure combine in one of the world's most individual destinations. With the world's second largest barrier reef, breathtaking relics from its Maya past and immersive wildlife experiences from birdwatching to searching for jaguars, it's no surprise that this pint-sized nation has become the place to go for relaxing vacationers and intrepid travellers alike.

THE MELTING POT OF THE AMERICAS

Belize was once a semi-secret destination – but word of the country's charms has got out, and everyone seems to want a piece of this bijou backwater now.

Often compared with Mexico and Costa Rica, the so-called Jewel of Central America is a distinct destination in its own right. From its wide variety of landscapes to the customs of the country's ethnic groups, Belize is almost defined by its lack of easy definition. It's a cultural conflation of Maya, Kriol, Garifuna and Mestizo people living side-by-side in seaside villages, rainforest towns and agricultural communities. This diversity makes Belize a welcoming place for tourists of all backgrounds.

Visitors wanting to help out and engage with local people and organisations can participate in a number of ways. Those interested in historical and cultural experiences can visit ancient ruins like Lamanai or take part in the Maya Village Homestay Network in southern Belize, a unique opportunity to become immersed in indigenous day-to-day activities, living in a Maya village and supporting the Maya people in their attempts to maintain their traditional way of life. Animal lovers can volunteer to walk shelter dogs at SAGA in San Pedro. And because resources can be hard to come by or expensive to ship, many resorts have programmes in which guests are given a list of needed goods to bring with them on their trip, helping children and animals to access essential items.

A CULTURE OF CONSERVATION

Despite differences in backgrounds and traditions, protecting the natural environment is a value that unites Belizeans: in 2018, marine conservation organisation Oceana facilitated a moratorium from the government on drilling for oil along the Belize Barrier Reef that remains

There's superb scuba diving along Belize's coast but watch for invasive lionfish.

HIGHLIGHTS

1 **Great Blue Hole** Dive into the depths of the Caribbean, seeing everything the Belize Barrier Reef has to offer.

2 **Actun Tunichil Muknal (ATM)** Take an expedition into these caves to see physical remains of the ancient Maya.

3 **Lamanai** Ancient Maya outpost accessible by boat.

4 **Silk Cayes** Castaway vibes permeate these far-off islands, where snorkelling brings you close to the abundant sea life.

5 **Belize Zoo** Meet Belizean animals often unable to return to their natural environment in this humane, educational zoo.

Green iguanas are a common sight in Belize's forests and waterways, here on the Rio Grande riverbank.

in effect; and in 2021 nearly 250,000 acres of primary-growth rainforest was purchased for perpetual protection. Plans were approved to phase out single-use plastics across the country too, and although the Covid-19 pandemic delayed this going into effect, Belize is still committed to making it happen.

For wildlife enthusiasts, it's consistent efforts from Belizean NGOs and local communities that have made the country such a prominent outdoor adventure destination. Visitors can easily see wild scarlet macaws, monkeys and crocodiles while exploring the jungle, and sea turtles, nurse sharks and manatees while snorkelling just about anywhere along the reef. Birdwatching is one of the most popular activities in the country due to the abundance of prime habitat still available for nearly 600 feathered species (90 of which are considered rare) to safely live, nest and migrate.

And most hotels in the country are family-owned, boutique accommodation, and are, by necessity, sustainable due to the realities of operating off-grid.

All that said, the rising popularity of Belize has led to projects unconcerned with environmental protections, including major cruise ship port operations that could significantly damage the marine ecosystem while making the tourist experience on shore more crowded. Overtourism is a problem on Belize's horizon, and it remains to be seen how the country will handle it.

POST-PANDEMIC PARADISE

Even as many countries felt the force of the pandemic and found themselves on Do Not Travel lists, Belize remained a relatively safe place to visit. However, with 50% of the country's GDP reliant on tourism and a big drop in arrivals, an economic crisis was inevitable.

The country is, though, well equipped to deal with a post-pandemic reality. Most restaurants are already open air to mitigate the Caribbean heat, and the majority of activities and attractions in the country are outdoors and socially distant by nature. With the exception of festivals and other large events, the tourist experience in Belize won't need to shift fundamentally from how it operated in the past.

And once travel is up and running again, Belize will be able to welcome guests from more destinations than ever. Airlines are expanding their services to the country and new hotels are opening to meet the increase in demand. Belize's secret is out and its future popularity looks promising, but that, hopefully, won't change the many reasons it has always been a magical, unique destination.

WHEN TO GO

DEC-APR
Dry season: expect sunny skies, warm days and occasional but brief showers.

JUN-OCT
Wet season: hot, with regular night time rainfall and potential hurricanes.

NOV & MAY
Very hot and humid, with irregular rainfall, more concentrated in May.

"Small in size and population, but rich in biodiversity, food and culture. Belize is a melting pot of unique ethnic groups and ecosystems, from mountains to jungles to sandy beaches."

DOYLE GARDINER
OWNER/OPERATOR OF DTOURZ AND
DOYLE'S SMOKE YAAD RESTAURANT

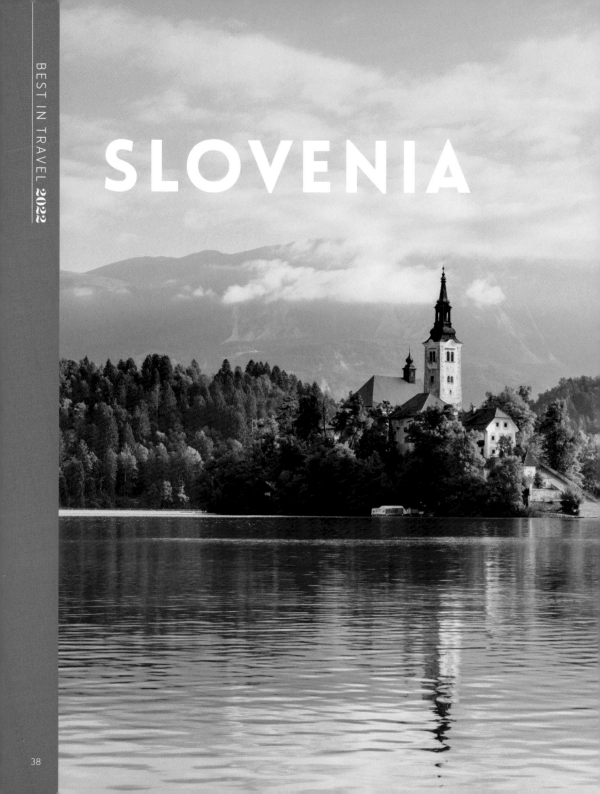

SLOVENIA

GOOD TO KNOW

UTC +1hr

Euro

Slovenian

Ljubljana Jože Pučnik Airport is Slovenia's main international airport. The main bus and train stations are also located in Ljubljana, the capital city.

• *A Farewell to Arms* Ernest Hemingway
• *The Land Between: A History of Slovenia* Oto Luthar (ed)
• *Slovenology: Living and Traveling in the World's Best Country* Noah Charney

If one word could describe Slovenia it would be green – literally and figuratively. Some two-thirds of this Central European nation is forested; and the 'Slovenia Green' eco certification, bestowed upon nearly 60 destinations here, is among the continent's most rigorous. Along with green credentials, this is also a place to come for unheralded wine and culinary prowess found in cities, towns and villages, strewn along hiking and cycling trails wedged between the Alps and the Adriatic.

RESPONSIBLE TRAVEL'S CRYSTAL BALL

It could be that Slovenians can see into the future. Or, more likely, they just care less about following trends than constructing their own narrative. Regardless of the reason, and with methodic focus, this small, mountainous land – surrounded by Italy, Austria, Hungary and Croatia – was busy becoming the industry's responsible-travel vanguard long before sustainability became a buzzword.

Ljubljana, Slovenia's capital, was named the European Green Capital in 2016 by the European Commission. In 2017, Slovenia was called 'the world's most sustainable country' after becoming the first entire nation to earn green certification by the Dutch organisation Green Destinations. In 2018, the Slovenian Tourist Board supported the planet's first entirely green cycling route, Bike Slovenia Green, with stops only in destinations certified sustainable. Then in 2020, to add to its embarrassment of riches,

the country's restaurants earned their first Michelin stars and Slovenian cyclists took the top podium places in the Tour de France.

By developing a tourism strategy that places quality over quantity and communities over consumerism, the country has unapologetically followed its own path and become a model for what many of today's travellers demand, but so rarely find: authenticity. That point was driven home in 2021 when Slovenia was hailed as the European Region of Gastronomy.

'When Slovenia committed to a quality-first strategy, the concept was counterintuitive to many,' says Jan Klavora, partner at Visit Good-Place, a Ljubljana-based eco-focused travel agency that certifies green destinations. 'But we know profits aren't the most important aspects of life. Keeping our residents happy and making sure Slovenia remains a great place to visit into the future is far more crucial.'

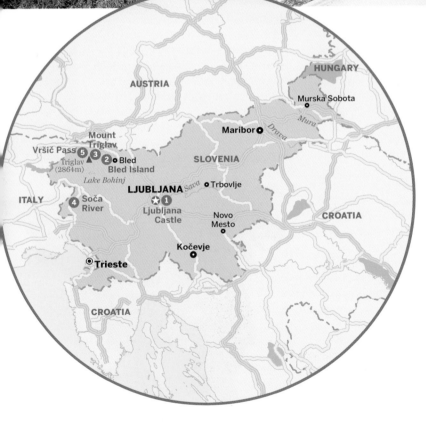

HIGHLIGHTS

1 Ljubljana Castle Above the capital's Old Town, with perfect bird's-eye city views.

2 Bled Island An iconic and beautiful Slovenian sight.

3 Mount Triglav Traditionally, every Slovene must climb the country's highest peak.

4 Soča River Emerald-green, clear and a cultural and adventure corridor for WWI history buffs, gastronomes, kayakers, hikers and cyclists.

5 Vršič Pass With 50 turns rising 1611m, this is the ride that explains how Slovenians have taken professional cycling by storm.

41

"Throughout our history, Slovenians have always been connected to the land as farmers. Because of this, our instinct is to protect our most important resource."

JANA APIH
DIRECTOR, GOODPLACE

COMMUNITY-BASED ROUTES SHOW THE WAY

Cycling along the new Bike Slovenia Green Gourmet Route, launched in June 2021, to the hilltop village of Šmartno in the Goriška Brda region, Slovenia unfolds in a way few countries can. Looking north, back up the path just pedalled, the snow-topped Julian Alps fill the skyline. To the south, you can already sense the sea as the Adriatic grows closer. Around you in every direction, vineyards cover the landscape, rolling to the horizon and dropping out of sight. The panorama is broken only by perched villages, where other cyclists are most likely also staring into the distance.

This Green Gourmet route – which, as the name implies, focuses on wine and food – takes cyclists to wineries, farms and Michelin-starred restaurants. The path's conceit is classically Slovenian in design and function: a microcosm of the nation's community-based tourism philosophy, which combines responsibility and practicality with a continual feast for the senses. Starting from Ljubljana, the itinerary heads west to Triglav National Park, passes the beautiful lakes of Bohinj

and Bled, takes in remote byways and forest roads along the Soča River's glacial waters, pedals through six wine-growing regions, and then rolls east to Maribor, straddling the Drava River. Like other routes in the Bike Slovenia Green category, its overnights are all green-certified stopovers.

In recent years, Slovenia has reaffirmed its position as travel's role model by creating a slew of such routes. The itineraries are meant to inspire independent travellers to access destinations at human speed. The purpose of the freely available route maps and information is to encourage self-locomotion,

WHEN TO GO

JUN-AUG
High season is sunny
and hot – and often
crowded.

**APR & MAY,
SEP & OCT**
The best time to be
outdoors, with fewer
tourists and cool but
sunny weather.

NOV-MAR
Ski season is
accompanied by
colder temperatures
and snow.

discourage automobile use and, by doing so, break up bottlenecks in popular resort areas.

There is, for instance, a path dedicated to hiking with history, the Walk of Peace, which follows WWI's front lines. There's the 267km Juliana Trail, a circular trek around Slovenia's tallest summit, 2864m-high Mount Triglav. And there's the Slovenia Green Capitals Route, a three-pronged cycling trail to the Kočevsko Region, the country's nature capital with Unesco-listed primeval forest; the Bela Krajina Region, the nation's cultural hub; and Ljubljana, the capital brimming with cafes, restaurants, shops and lounge bars.

Slovenia is that rare combination of affordable, beautiful, ancient and outdoor-leaning. Its sensibility and traditions embrace the role of host but put its citizens first. All this and it is conveniently located in the heart of Europe, making it an easily accessible destination for travellers wanting to take a wonderful walk on the green side.

Above: Piran, a Venetian-Gothic gem sitting pretty on Slovenia's Adriatic coast.

Left: grimacing gargoyles decorate Ljubljana's much-loved Dragon Bridge.

Previous spread: the Logar Valley in winter.

06

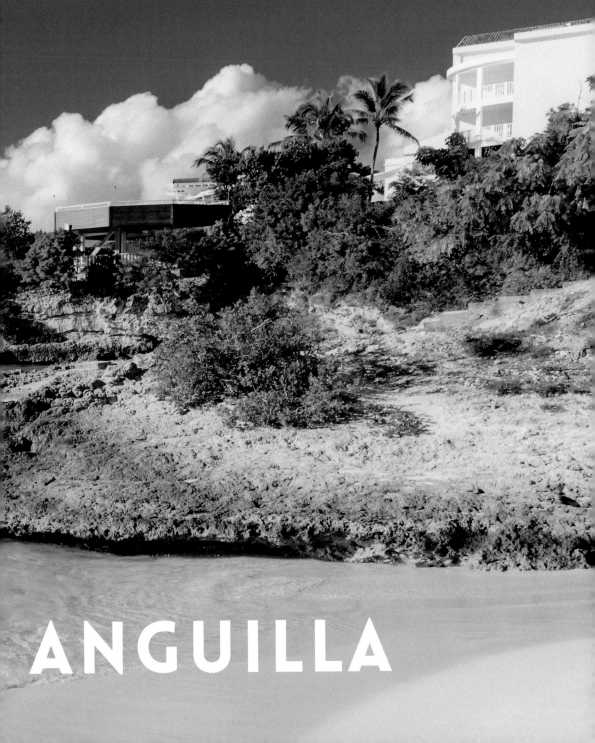

ANGUILLA

© PREVIOUS PAGE: SHUTTERSTOCK | DIEGOMARIOTTINI; ABOVE: NIKOLAY TRANOV | SHUTTERSTOCK

GOOD TO KNOW

UTC -4hr

Eastern Caribbean Dollar

English

The nearest international airport is on the neighbouring island of St Maarten, a 30-minute ferry ride from Anguilla.

📖

• *Anguilla: Tranquil Isle of the Caribbean* Colville Petty and Brenda Carty
• *A Trip to the Beach* Melinda and Robert Blanchard
• *Under an English Heaven* Donald E. Westlake

Look out the plane window as you're descending over the shimmering Caribbean and you'll see how this long, skinny island got its name – Anguilla comes from the Latin for 'eel'. Visitors come to discover its sinuous lengths by bike or scooter, snorkel its psychedelic reefs, laze on pink-tinged beaches, delve into its historic ruins and join locals for evening barbecues. Serious about sustainability, Anguilla's not the place for mega-resort lounging, but for low-key, eco-friendly exploration.

A TOUGH FIVE YEARS

The last half-decade has not been easy for Anguilla. In September 2017, Hurricane Irma slammed into the low-lying island as a Category 5 storm – some 90% of houses were damaged and infrastructure was devastated. Faced with such destruction and similar future events due to climate change, islanders came together and committed to rebuilding sustainably. New initiatives include phasing out single-use plastics, incentivising renewable energy projects and building a hurricane-resistant greenhouse to provide the island with secure, locally grown food.

But just a few years after Irma, Covid-19 ravaged the tourism industry a second time (though early government action on the virus kept national cases to a minimum). As it opens up to visitors again, Anguilla is aiming to stake a claim as a place to enjoy a more relaxed, greener, slower-paced travel experience. But what exactly does that mean?

HOW TO TRAVEL, ANGUILLA-STYLE

It means exploring the island by the most eco-friendly of vehicles – the good old bike. Just 25km long and virtually flat, Anguilla is ideal for cycling. Start at Shoal Bay East, a 3km stretch of sand so white and sparkling it looks like crushed diamonds. Fringed by palms and sea grape, it's a scenic location for a morning dip. Meads Bay means lunch and, if you're lucky, a chance to spy dolphins in the clear waters. Don't miss the new public viewing platform at Meads Bay Pond, a prime waterbird-watching site. Rest the calves a while at Barnes Bay, a secluded beach whose iguana-shaped rock formation is Instagram gold, and wind up at Maundays Bay, pedalling across a bridge over the salt pond to sink your toes into the sand as the sun sets.

It also means getting to know the history of Anguilla's indigenous inhabitants. Start at the Heritage Collection Museum in East End Village, where local historian

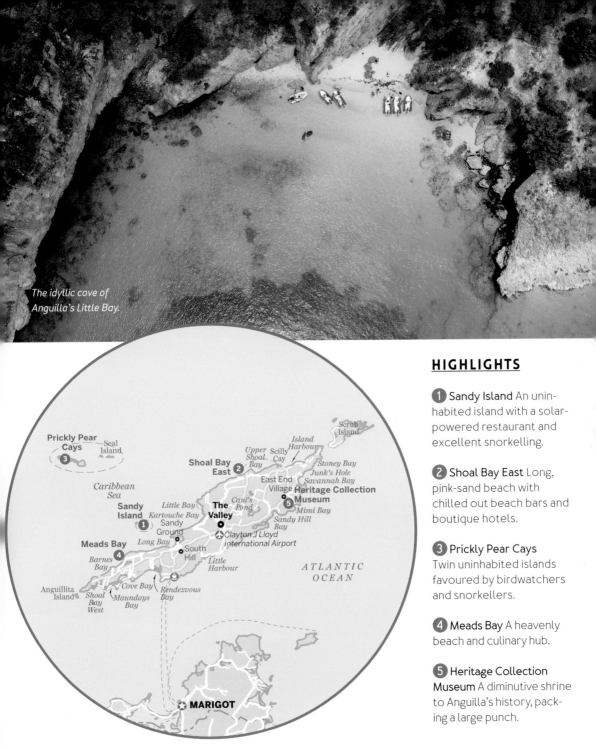

The idyllic cove of Anguilla's Little Bay.

47

HIGHLIGHTS

1 Sandy Island An uninhabited island with a solar-powered restaurant and excellent snorkelling.

2 Shoal Bay East Long, pink-sand beach with chilled out beach bars and boutique hotels.

3 Prickly Pear Cays Twin uninhabited islands favoured by birdwatchers and snorkellers.

4 Meads Bay A heavenly beach and culinary hub.

5 Heritage Collection Museum A diminutive shrine to Anguilla's history, packing a large punch.

Map labels:
Prickly Pear Cays — Seal Island
Caribbean Sea
Sandy Island
Little Bay
Kartouche Bay
Sandy Ground
Long Bay
Meads Bay
Barnes Bay
Anguillita Island
Shoal Bay West
Cove Bay
Maundays Bay
Rendezvous Bay
South Hill
Little Harbour
The Valley
Caul's Pond
Shoal Bay East
Upper Shoal Bay
Scilly Cay
Island Harbour
Scrub Island
East End Village
Stoney Bay
Junk's Hole
Savannah Bay
Heritage Collection Museum
Mimi Bay
Sandy Hill
Sandy Bay
Clayton J Lloyd International Airport
ATLANTIC OCEAN
MARIGOT

Sprinkled with fragrant local nutmeg, Anguilla's signature rum punch is best enjoyed beachside.

Colville Petty curates artefacts dating back to the Arawaks. The Arawak people arrived on the island, which they called Malliouhana, around 4000 years ago, and once populated some 40 villages. Centuries later, in 1650, Anguilla was colonised by the English, who used enslaved Africans to grow sugarcane; the descendants of these enslaved people make up the majority of today's population. From the museum, history buffs can follow the Anguilla Heritage Trail, stopping at ancient Amerindian sites, plantations built by enslaved people and a colonial courthouse and factory.

And it means hopping on a boat to the Prickly Pear Cays, a pair of uninhabited islands in Anguilla's protected Marine Park. Endangered hawksbill and green sea turtles lay their eggs on Prickly Pear East, while a colony of brown pelicans nests in the scrub on windswept Prickly Pear West. The Cays make for a full-day trip, complete with lunch at the restaurant on Prickly Pear East, where you can rent snorkel gear for a lazy afternoon of gazing at crayon-coloured fish, or try your hand at paddleboarding on the glassy waters. For a similar castaway vibe, seek out Sandy Island, a speck of white sand with a beach bar, accessible by speedboat from the village of Sandy Ground.

It means eating at places like Blanchard's Restaurant and Beach Shack, where local organic produce is served on compostable plates.

The restaurant became a relief centre after Hurricane Irma and a community food pantry during the pandemic. Order plantain chips, Thai red curry mussels and grilled Anguilla crayfish, chased with a flight of aged Caribbean rums.

And the final box to check on your sustainable, immersive Anguilla expedition is sleeping at a boutique hotel or rental condo rather than the massive all-inclusive resort that many have come to expect of the Caribbean. Sure, there are big-brand luxury properties here, but the general vibe is laid-back and discreet. You may spot a celeb, but there's no paparazzi or velvet ropes. A top sustainable pick is Frangipani Beach Resort at Meads Bay, whose new solar panel system powers 70% of the property.

Anguilla might not have the name recognition of its Caribbean neighbours, but its calm, in-harmony-with-the-ecosystem approach to tourism may in fact put it at the cutting edge of future travel.

WHEN TO GO

DEC-APR
Clear skies and plenty of visitors escaping colder climes.

MAY-AUG
Anguilla's humid summer sees smaller crowds and lower prices.

SEP-NOV
Hurricane season, a cheaper – though risky – time to visit.

"My favourite thing about Anguilla, aside from stunning beaches, is the wildlife. From nesting sea turtles to a wide variety of bird species, nature provides gifts every day."

JACKIE CESTERO
OWNER, NATURE EXPLORERS ANGUILLA

OMAN

07

GOOD TO KNOW

UTC +4hr

Omani rial

Arabic (English widely spoken).

Oman has three international airports, Muscat International being the main one. Cruise liners call in at Khasab, Sohar, Muscat and Salalah.

• www.timesofoman.com
• *The Turtle of Oman* Naomi Shihab Nye
• *Omani Folktales* Hatim Al Taie and Joan Pickersgill

Oman is a land of wild, open deserts, vast mountain ranges, a shimmering coastline and vibrant cities, a place where all that is alluring about Arabia comes to life in spectacular fashion. As the world opens up again, the country's current locals-focused tourism options and long-term sustainable strategies make it a prime destination for those looking to experience a progressive Gulf destination with a strong cultural heritage.

OMANI RENAISSANCE

Less than 50 years ago, Oman had only two schools, two missionary hospitals, barely a paved road and lay ravaged by civil war. For a nation that was once a seafaring superpower with outposts in Africa, India and Pakistan, this was a tragedy.

Then came a renaissance under the recently deceased Sultan Qaboos who immediately abolished slavery and made Omani women the first in the Gulf to hold positions of high office. He introduced a culture of tolerance that saw churches and temples built in the deeply Ibadi Muslim nation; schools, universities and hospitals were opened across the sultanate; and highways linked new airports and seaports with Oman's growing towns and cities. Slowly, just as in antiquity, people and merchandise from across the globe began coming back to Oman. Best of all, this was achieved while perfectly balancing the nation's rich heritage with all the demands of a modern Gulf society.

A COUNTRY OF CONTRASTS

Head to the Musandam Peninsula in the north and you can board a dhow to explore the country's beautiful deep-blue fjord-like *khors* (estuaries) that have led to the region being dubbed the 'Norway of Arabia'. Take an off-road drive through the Hajar Mountains, home to Oman's highest peaks and its deepest canyon, Wadi Nakhr. The gateway to this is the city of Nizwa with a wonderful walled souk and giant fort, surrounded by a thick palm oasis.

As the mountains' gentle slopes embrace the Gulf of Oman, they become the backdrop to the country's bustling ancient capital, Muscat, which has forgone the high-rises of neighbouring Gulf capitals in favour of traditional domed structures and arabesque windows. As well as the traditional, the city is also home to state-of-the-art museums, modern art galleries and even an opera house, all of which rub shoulders with ancient souks and the stunning

HIGHLIGHTS

① **Mutrah Souk** Lose yourself in the labyrinthine alleys of Muscat's bazaar.

② **Ras Al Jinz** One of the most important nesting sites for endangered green turtles.

③ **Bahla Fort** Enjoy panoramic views of the medieval Islamic settlement of Bahla from this Unesco World Heritage Site.

④ **Dhofar** A subtropical region that was once an ancient trade centre for frankincense, gold and myrrh.

⑤ **Wadi Shab** Swim in turquoise pools and beneath cooling waterfalls.

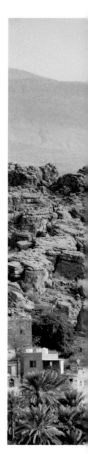

> **"Oman's transformation has been exhilarating: steady and sympathetic to our long history and status as one of the Middle East's most culturally significant states."**
>
> SAID SALIM RASHID AL-MAAWALI
> PUBLISHER, FM MAGAZINE

Sultan Qaboos mosque, home to a Persian carpet woven by 600 women over four years.

Moving down towards the Arabian Sea's coastline, you'll find one of the world's most important nesting sites for the endangered green turtle. Here, on the beaches of the Ras Al Jinz Turtle Reserve, you can join a night tour to watch some of the 20,000 or so females that return annually to lay their eggs in the same sands in which they themselves were born. Head south for the wild dunes of the Sharqiyah Sands and the subtropical expanse at the edge of the Empty Quarter before entering the spectacular Dhofar region, where just after the November to March rainy season the entire landscape goes from dusty brown to an iridescent green. A world away from the cosmopolitan and industrial north, here the regional capital of Salalah offers a glimpse of Oman's former territory of Zanzibar, thanks to coconut-fringed beaches and banana plantations.

PLANNING FOR A SUSTAINABLE FUTURE

Oman's long history as a trade and cultural crossroads is informing its plans for the future. The country's Vision 2040 is a progressive project that, among other initiatives, places community and sustainability at the centre of its tourism strategy.

Whether you're sipping a *karak chai* (a drink that recalls the nation's historic maritime links to the sub-continent) or a cardamom-infused *kahva* (which harks back to Oman's desert roots), you'll soon be enjoying it from a paper rather than a plastic cup – a drive to ban single-use plastic began at the

WHEN TO GO

NOV-MAR
Balmy days make this the tourist high season.

JUN-AUG
This is peak summer when temperatures soar – best avoided.

APRIL & MAY, SEP & OCT
Shoulder months with bearable temperatures.

start of 2021. And such is Oman's multinational mix, the vendor is as likely to greet you in Baluchi, Swahili, Malayalam or Tagalog as in the native Arabic.

Low-impact trips focused on locals and their way of life have become a big thing here. Some Omanis are trained to welcome tourists. Some are encouraged to renovate their old mud-brick ancestral home, making homestays for travellers to visit. Others are learning to host cooking lessons that teach foreigners how to make Omani-favourites like *harees* (a type of chicken porridge) or to lead guided foraging walks that show visitors where to find the herbs that have long been a part of traditional Omani culture.

Seeing its domestic population as key to the success of tourism development means that, unlike its wealthy neighbours, modest oil-income Oman not only needs visitors, it deserves them.

Above: mountain-hugging Misfat Al Abriyyin is one of Oman's iconic sights.

Left: from a cardamom-scented cup of kahva *to a sugar-hit slice of* kanafeh, *Omani cuisine promises delightful discoveries.*

Previous spread: inside Nakhal Fort.

NEPAL

GOOD TO KNOW

UTC +5hr 30min

Nepali rupee

Nepali

Kathmandu has global flight connections through India, Southeast Asia and the Gulf. New international airports under construction in the Terai and at Pokhara are due to complete in 2022.

• *Arresting God in Kathmandu* Samrat Upadhyay
• *The Tutor of History* Manjushree Thapa
• *Mountains Painted with Turmeric* Lil Bahadur Chettri

When it comes to getting away from it all, you can't get much farther than the high passes of the Himalaya and the place most associated with them, Nepal. The country is the front door to the world's tallest peaks, a spectacular playground for trekkers, climbers and adventurers. Connecting through the captivating, cultured capital, Kathmandu, new arrivals can be out on the trails within hours, social distancing the natural way in a Himalayan wonderland of mountains and monasteries.

THE WORLD'S GREATEST ESCAPE

After the ravages of Covid-19, personal space is the travel must-have for 2022, and Nepal delivers on an epic scale. An astonishing 75% of the country is covered by mountains, and huge areas are accessible only on foot or via internal flights that weave between the peaks. Once you leave the busy townships of the Terai plains and Kathmandu Valley, the human population dwindles. Above the snowline, particularly in the wild east and west of the country, there could be a whole valley between you and the next human being.

Even better, escaping a crowd is easier here than almost anywhere else in Asia, thanks to Nepal's world-class trekking infrastructure. Soon after landing in Kathmandu, you can be far from the crush of humanity in a landscape with more yaks and yetis (if you believe in that sort of thing) than people. Skip the famous trekking routes around Everest and Annapurna and you'll even leave other trekkers behind. On the trails around Kanchenjunga in the east and Dolpo and Humla in the west, you could have mesmerising, inspiring mountain panoramas almost entirely to yourself – an uplifting, elemental experience.

MAXIMUM VARIETY

Tucked between India and China, tiny Nepal sits in the shadow of giants, but what it lacks in size, it makes up for in wonders. You probably already have a picture in your mind of pagoda-roofed temples, monks chanting mantras in mountain monasteries and empty trekking routes straining over snow-dusted passes. And that's all here in Nepal, along with a dizzying diversity of landscapes, a living museum of medieval monuments and a fascinating fusion of Hindu and Buddhist culture and customs, combining to create the perfect antidote to the stresses of the modern age. There's nowhere in the world that offers quite so much

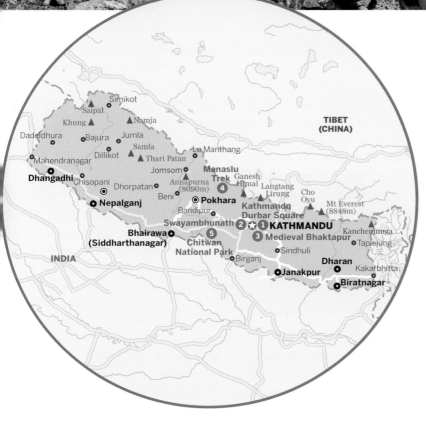

Yaks carry cargo in the Himalayan mountains.

HIGHLIGHTS

1 Kathmandu Durbar Square The heart of Nepal's medieval capital, crammed with palaces, temples and pagodas.

2 Swayambhunath Climb monkey-crowded steps to approach this 'self-arisen' stupa, soaring over Kathmandu.

3 Medieval Bhaktapur The most evocative of Kathmandu Valley's historic city-states.

4 Manaslu Trek Nepal's best new trekking destination; the grandeur of Annapurna and Everest without the crowds.

5 Chitwan National Park Accessible lowland park home to elephants, tigers and rhinos.

Chitwan National Park offers a good chance of spotting Nepal's greater one-horned rhinos.

variety – tigers and temples, silent meditation and frenetic festivals, jungles and mountain moonscapes – in such a compact space.

A NATION FINDING ITS CONFIDENCE

For most of the 20th century, Nepal was more famous for the achievements of foreign mountaineers – Edmund Hillary, Reinhold Messner, Dave Hahn and the like – than for the incredible work done by local climbers, but things are changing fast. The world's top mountaineering records are now falling to young Nepali climbers such as Nirmal 'Nims' Purja, who climbed Earth's fourteen mountains over 8000m in just six months, beating the previous record by an astonishing seven years and leaving the rest of the world looking on in awe and admiration.

In the century since the foundation of diplomatic ties with Britain – which saved Nepal from colonial conquest – this tiny Himalayan nation has also forged ahead with social change. In contrast with neighbouring countries which have suppressed LGBT+ rights, Nepal proudly embraced them, enshrining equality in the constitution and becoming one of the first countries to allow legal self-determination for trans people. Although challenges remain, Nepal is also taking commendable steps towards gender equality – in 2021, six Nepali women reached the 8091m summit of Annapurna I, rocking local perceptions of climbing as a male-only pursuit.

PRESERVING THE HIMALAYA

With challenges ranging from earthquakes to melting glaciers, conservation and preservation are firmly on the agenda in Nepal. Money from visitors has a vital role to play in restoring the medieval temples and townships damaged in the devastating 2015 quake, while the popularity of safari tourism has helped the country buck global trends by having growing populations of tigers and rhinos in the jungles of the Terai. Swapping harmful elephant rides for guided walks with elephants in the country's national parks is one more way travellers can have a positive impact on how tourism develops here in the future.

Visitors who hike into Nepal's mountains have a unique opportunity to make a difference, too. Independent trekkers can arrange porters and guides on arrival in the mountains, sleeping and eating in local teahouses to steer money directly to local communities. Do your bit to help preserve Nepal's empty spaces and promote a sustainable tourist industry by walking into the mountains rather than flying to the trailheads, and carrying out litter – both yours and other people's – at the end of your trek.

WHEN TO GO

OCT & NOV
The post-monsoon trekking season brings warm walking weather and clear mountain vistas.

JUN-SEP, DEC-FEB
The sultry summer sees views obscured by monsoon rain-clouds; winter brings heavy snow to the trails.

MAR-MAY
The post-winter trekking season sees warming temperatures and blooming rhododendrons in the mountains.

> "Nothing can replace the restorative nature of time spent in the Nepali wilderness, with good people, good food, a dose of camping and the company of Mother Nature."

ROBIN SHRESTHA
TOURIST AGENCY MANAGER

MALAWI

GOOD TO KNOW

UTC +2hr

Malawian kwacha

English (official), plus
Chichewa (most com-
mon), Lomwe, Yao,
Ngoni, Tumbuka, Sena
and others.

Lilongwe and Blantyre
have connections to
airports in South Af-
rica, Kenya, Tanzania
and Ethiopia. Malawi is
also a staging post for
overland trucks head-
ing between Nairobi
and Cape Town.

• *For Honour* Stanley
Onjezani Kenani
• *The Boy Who
Harnessed the Wind*
William Kamkwamba
and Bryan Mealer
• *The Lower River* Paul
Theroux

Trailblazing conservation work has added wildlife-watching to the appeal of this small African country with a huge lake and hugely likeable locals. Malawi was already popular as a safe and friendly intro to Africa, with multi-coloured cichlid fish in its eponymous lake, reggae-loving beach towns, mountaintop mission stations, hiking trails and tea plantations. Now it's added safaris to its list of credentials, thanks to the pioneering revival of its three major wildlife reserves by the NGO African Parks.

NEW LIFE IN THE AFRICAN BUSH
In recent years, 'the warm heart of Africa', as Malawi is often called, has become one of the continent's most fully rounded wildlife destinations. Majete Wildlife Reserve in the south now has the complete Big Five (leopard, lion, buffalo, elephant and rhinoceros). In the east, Liwonde National Park offers unbeatable river-based wildlife-watching. And central Nkhotakota Wildlife Reserve has seen the historic translocation of more than 520 elephants and 2000 other animals from Majete and Liwonde thanks to the efforts of media-savvy African Parks, which enlisted its president, British Royal Prince Harry, to spend three weeks anaesthetising and affixing radio collars in 2017. More recently, the NGO flew 17 critically endangered black rhinos from South Africa to Liwonde, one of the largest international rhino relocations ever, following similar journeys by cheetahs to Majete and Liwonde – the cats' first appearance in either park for 20 years.

Guided by five pillars (biodiversity conservation, community development, tourism, law enforcement and management), African Parks has brought new life to Malawi's formerly poached-out bush, the results of which can be seen everywhere from the six rhino calves born after the relocation to the job opportunities now available in impoverished rural areas. The up-and-coming reserves encourage investment by other tourism businesses, such as the latest addition to Robin Pope Safaris' portfolio of chic lodges, Kuthengo Camp – four safari tents among the fever trees and baobabs by the Shire River in Liwonde.

The story of job creation combining conservation and travel continues at Tongole Wilderness Lodge in Nkhotakota. The solar-powered lodge created 100 jobs in the construction of its thatched main building and suites, which blend in with the riverside *miombo*

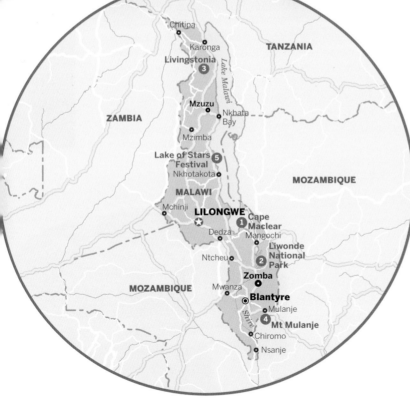

HIGHLIGHTS

1 **Cape Maclear** Relax on the beach or kayak to nearby Domwe and Mumbo islands.

2 **Liwonde National Park** One of Africa's best river-based wildlife-watching destinations.

3 **Livingstonia** Stay at an eco-lodge on the escarpment edge and visit the crumbling Scottish mission station.

4 **Mt Mulanje** Hike in the granite massif fringed with tea plantations, and the Nyika, Zomba and Viphya plateaus.

5 **Lake of Stars Festival** Three days of African music and mellow vibes, held at beach lodges every September.

> **"Malawi is off the beaten path, but this just lends itself to the local vibes, hidden gems and welcoming spirit that the small country shares with all."**
>
> KATLYN SALEY
> CO-OWNER, MUSHROOM FARM, LIVINGSTONIA

(woodland) in one of Malawi's least-developed wildernesses, and it continues to train and employ some 30 locals, including the guides on its low-impact canoe and walking safaris. In one of the world's poorest countries, the average tourist employee supports at least 14 people, and the Tongole Foundation extends the lodge's positive impact through maintaining schools, distributing mosquito nets to prevent infant deaths from malaria, and reducing poaching though education.

GREENING POST-PANDEMIC TOURISM

The closure of international borders during the Covid-19 pandemic severely affected an economy that relies heavily on tourism and aid workers, but Malawi is ready to responsibly welcome travellers again, with a Safe Travels Stamp from the World Travel & Tourism Council (WTTC). During the lull, myriad lodges, ranging from island hideaways to beachfront backpacker hangouts, busied themselves with eco-tourist projects. Dzalanyama Forest Lodge, near capital Lilongwe, launched new forest walks, mountain-biking trails

and leafy bathing areas, while Blue Zebra Island Lodge on Nankoma Island replaced its generator with solar power, established a rangers base camp to prevent illegal fishing, expanded its nature trails and opened a lakeside spa beneath an ancient fig tree.

With around 90% of Malawians relying on firewood and charcoal for cooking and heating, Blue Zebra and Likoma Island's dreamy Kaya Mawa resort stepped up reforestation of their respective islands – the latter's Green Safaris Conservation Foundation planted more than 7000 saplings, sharing knowledge to nurture eco-minded islanders. Even

WHEN TO GO

SEP & OCT
The end of the dry season sees lower humidity and temperatures.

NOV-APR
The rainy season, with hot and steamy weather.

MAY-AUG
The dry season, with the coolest temperatures, fastest lake winds, highland frost and dank chiperone mist.

in the Malawian capital, Lilongwe Wildlife Trust launched Project GreenHeart to overhaul its 180-acre forest reserve, wildlife rescue and welfare facility, with the aim of ultimately creating an ecological corridor through the city.

WARM WATERS, WARM WELCOME
Alongside exciting developments in the parks and reserves, there's long-established biodiverse Lake Malawi to enjoy too, where sunny days can be spent swimming among shoals of cichlids and dozing in a hammock. Known as the 'calendar lake' for being 365 miles long, 52 miles wide and fed by 12 rivers, this Unesco-protected watery Serengeti is one of the world's best freshwater diving destinations, with operators in Nkhata Bay and Cape Maclear. You'll see many of the 1000-plus species inhabiting Africa's third-largest lake, more than in any other inland body of water in the world.

Whichever adventures you choose, Malawians are ready to show off their multifaceted country.

Above: African elephant populations are on the rise in Malawi with the translocation of more than 520 animals to Nkhotakota Wildlife Reserve.

Left: job creation is central to the travel and conservation strategy of Malawi NGO African Parks.

Previous spread: Cape Maclear on Lake Malawi.

EGYPT

10

GOOD TO KNOW

UTC +2hr

Egyptian Pound

Arabic

Cairo International Airport is Egypt's main air hub.

• *Taxi* Khaled Alkhamissi
• *The Yacoubian Building* Alaa Al Aswany
• *The Cairo Trilogy* Naguib Mahfouz

In 1922, Howard Carter's search for a then little-known pharaoh resulted in one of the most famous archaeological finds of all time. Egypt is gearing up to commemorate the 100 year anniversary of the discovery of Tutankhamun's tomb with a flurry of new museums that celebrate the country's cultural riches. But away from the temples and tombs, grassroots tourism start-ups are also making waves, reflecting an Egypt far removed from pyramids and ancient pharaonic glories.

NEW HOMES FOR ANCIENT TREASURES

2022 is a triple anniversary year. Along with the centenary of Carter's discovery, it's also 100 years since the Kingdom of Egypt was created (beginning the road to full independence), and Egyptology will commemorate the 200 year anniversary of French hieroglyph expert Champollion cracking the Rosetta Stone. For tourism though, 2022's all about Tutankhamun. Egypt's hoping to mark the occasion with the much-delayed Grand Egyptian Museum (GEM) in Giza flinging open its doors to become the new home for the young pharaoh's grave-goods bounty.

While the GEM's will-it-won't-it opening grabs headlines, in the background a host of museums and monument restorations have already been completed. Sohag and Sharm El-Sheikh have both opened long-awaited museums, while in Cairo, 2020 saw the eccentric Baron Empain Palace finally restored, followed by the 2021 full opening of the National Museum of Egyptian Civilization (NMEC).

There's never been a shortage of fascinating objects to fill all these museums – but archaeologists have continued digging up more ancient prizes to add to the pile anyway. Outside the capital, the sands of Saqqara have surrendered a steady stream of riches recently, and on Luxor's west bank the major find of 30 coloured coffins at Al-Asasif in 2019 was only topped by 2021's discovery of a town from Pharaoh Amenhotep III's time (around 3400 years ago).

As the major museum shakeup gathered pace, in April 2021 Egypt pulled off an artefact move that will probably never be beaten for pomp and splendour. The Royal Mummies collection left their old digs at Tahrir Square's Egyptian Museum and travelled to their new home at NMEC via a dramatic parade through central Cairo's streets. It was rightly a moment of national pride – and a not-too-subtle reminder to

Pillars and heiro-glyphics at Karnak temple in Luxor.

HIGHLIGHTS

1 **Luxor** Open-air museum of giant temples and tombs covered in vivid murals.

2 **Cairo** The core harbours incredible Islamic architecture; the outskirts hold pyramids you may have heard of.

3 **Nile cruising** Hemmed in by desert, the date-palm-lined banks of the Nile are Egypt at its most lush.

4 **Ras Mohammed** Colourful reefs rated among the world's top dive sites.

5 **White Desert National Park** Weird, white, wind-sculpted rock spires marooned in a sea of sand.

71

Hop on board a traditional Egyptian felucca to cruise the Nile in style.

the world that few can match Egypt's depth of history and heritage.

AWAY FROM THE TEMPLES AND TOMBS

Increasingly, Egypt is about more than just its past. While pharaonic riches continue to be the calling-card, community-based tourism and niche tours that eschew the monument checklist are beginning to take off.

In Cairo, entrepreneurial food fans Laila Hassaballa and Mariam Nezar have gained international media attention for their company Bellies En-Route, which runs street-eats walking tours of the city. This local-focused style of tourism has long been missing from Egypt's capital and offers a ground-level introduction to Cairo very different to the typical museum-hop and Giza Pyramids visit most tourists limit themselves to.

Meanwhile, Egypt's rugged desert mountain landscapes have never been more accessible thanks to the country's two long-distance trekking trails. Opened in 2015, the Sinai Trail blazed the way and has steadily expanded, now incorporating 550km of trail. Run by eight of the Sinai Peninsula's Bedouin tribes, it has both provided work for local Bedouin, stimulating village economies, and been a catalyst for inter-tribal cooperation and a resurgence of Bedouin culture.

Thanks to the Sinai Trail's success, the Red Sea Mountain Trail soon followed with a 170km circuit-trekking route across the Red Sea coast's barren heartland. This sister trail is operated by the local Maaza Bedouin tribe, in keeping with the community-focused ethos behind the Sinai Trail.

EGYPTIAN TOURISM TODAY

All of this is welcome news in a country where bad news has a habit of overshadowing anything positive. Since 2011 Egypt has been trying to build back its tourism economy to pre-revolution levels but has suffered several setbacks. The ongoing insurgency in North Sinai and a number of horrific terrorist attacks have kept many would-be travellers away, as has President Sisi's continuing crackdown on journalists, campaigners and other voices of opposition.

This tourism crisis has exacerbated the economic problems of many Egyptians who work in hospitality, at a time when rampant inflation has caused living standards to slip. A recent World Bank report stated that 60% of Egyptians now live in poverty. In 2019, Egypt's visitor numbers had finally begun to look rosy once again. Then Covid-19 hit and the tourists disappeared. 2022's anniversaries are the boost everyone involved in Egypt's travel industry is hoping will kick tourism back into high gear. And there's no lack of incredible old and new sights awaiting those who do return.

WHEN TO GO

NOV-FEB
Mostly blue skies and mostly warm, though chilly after dark.

JUN-AUG
Temperature levels zoom up to scorching during summer.

MAR-MAY & SEP-OCT
Not as uncomfortably hot as summer. Occasional dust storms in spring.

> "The Sinai Trail helps the Bedouin preserve traditional culture, teach our youth about the desert and create work opportunities in the mountains where no tourists used to come."

NASSER MANSOUR, JEBELEYA TRIBE HEAD GUIDE, SINAI TRAIL

TOP
10
CITIES

AUCKLAND, NEW ZEALAND

GOOD TO KNOW

UTC +12hr

New Zealand dollar

English, Māori, NZ Sign Language

Auckland International Airport is New Zealand's main transport hub.

• *Nights in the Gardens of Spain* Witi Ihimaera
• *Under the Mountain* Maurice Gee
• *Rangatira* Paula Morris

Set on an isthmus between two harbours at the narrowest point of New Zealand's North Island, Auckland is unique. Within the city's boundaries there are 53 volcanoes, more than 50 islands, three wine regions and numerous beaches. The country's biggest and most diverse city has always been beautiful, but one unpredicted consequence of Covid-19 has been the blossoming of Auckland's cultural scene, putting a fresh spotlight on exciting local creativity.

TREASURES TO SEEK OUT

In Māori, Auckland is known as Tāmaki Makaurau (Tāmaki of a hundred lovers) – a fitting name, as it's the area's considerable natural assets that have had suitors fighting over it for centuries. That said, Auckland isn't the most immediately obvious tourist destination. If there was ever a metropolis that benefitted from a good guidebook or a local to show you around, this is it. Wandering aimlessly in the city centre just isn't going to give you a sense of why it regularly lands near or at the top of the world's most liveable cities list. For that you are going to need to hire a car or jump on a ferry.

Head west and you'll find lush rainforest and wild surf beaches buffeted by the Tasman Sea. Head north and there are geothermal springs, wineries and yet more rainforest and beaches. To the east the island-studded Hauraki Gulf glistens, home to resident populations of whales, dolphins and penguins, sanctuaries sheltering some of the world's rarest birds, and more notable wineries on Waiheke.

EMBRACING LOCAL TALENT

New Zealand's 'go hard and go early' elimination approach to Covid-19 meant that, outside of a handful of relatively short lockdowns, life swiftly returned to something approaching normal. As a result, Auckland suddenly found itself in the position of being perhaps the most vibrant city in the world, with restaurants, galleries, theatres, concerts and large sporting events all in full swing. It was never going to stay at the top but the repercussions of this unexpected, inward-gazing moment continue to reverberate through Auckland's cultural life.

When the borders closed, the spotlight turned to homegrown talent, and Kiwi culture is now being recognised and supported in a way that it seldom has been before. Events such as the record-breaking

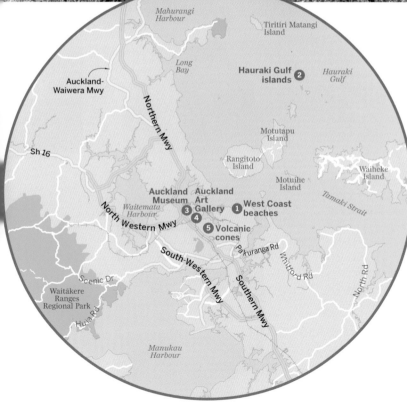

HIGHLIGHTS

1 **West Coast beaches**
Pounding surf, black sand, rainforest, waterfalls and wildlife.

2 **Hauraki Gulf islands**
Taste wine on Waiheke and spot endangered birds on Tiritiri Matangi.

3 **Auckland Museum** A superlative collection of Māori and Pasifika artefacts in a striking building.

4 **Auckland Art Gallery**
City highlight with New Zealand and global works.

5 **Volcanic cone climbs**
Spectacular views of the city, harbour and islands.

> ## "Waiheke is known as Auckland's island of wine. Its amazing terroir combined with great local winemakers is making it a force to be reckoned with."

RACHAEL CARTER
FOUNDER, SOHO WINES

Six60 gig at Auckland's Eden Park in 2021 attracted 50,000 people, the largest-ever audience for an NZ act, and have kindled a confidence in the local music scene that looks set to continue, even as a slew of international acts have rushed to reschedule their Covid-cancelled gigs to 2022.

Since the start of the pandemic, the country's long-lamented 'brain drain' – which historically saw the best and the brightest departing to seek their fortunes overseas – has turned into a 'brain gain', with New Zealanders flooding back to the relative safety of their homeland. A case in point is Peter Gordon, a New Zealand-born chef of Māori descent, who made his name in London as one of the pioneers of fusion cuisine. He and his partner Alastair Carruthers returned near the beginning of the pandemic and went on to set up Homeland – a restaurant, cooking school and showcase for sustainable food producers from across Aotearoa (the Māori name for the country) and the Pacific. Inspired by the proverb 'Nā tō rourou, nā taku rourou ka ora ai te iwi' (With your food basket and my food basket the people will thrive), the cooking school hosts days on which migrant communities are invited to come along to share and celebrate their food culture.

Auckland's big Polynesian population (the largest of any city in the world) means Māori and Pasifika culture infuses its entire creative sphere. The more traditional side is showcased in the huge annual Polyfest and Pasifika festivals, while

WHEN TO GO

DEC-MAR
The sunniest, warmest and driest months, but also the most humid.

APR & SEP-NOV
Mild to cool temperatures and a moderate chance of rain.

MAY-AUG
Winter sees some frosty mornings and lots of rain.

an underground edge is represented by the Polyswagg hip-hop dance style of choreographer-to-the-stars Parris Goebel, and FAFSWAG, an avant-garde performing arts collective created by and starring the city's queer Pasifika youth.

AUCKLAND IN 2022

The biggest event on the city's 2022 calendar is the Women's Rugby World Cup, rescheduled from 2021 due to the pandemic and highly anticipated by local fans – the national team, the Black Ferns, have won five of the last six tournaments and it's expected that, if they reach the final, the match will draw the largest crowds ever for the women's game.

As its period of involuntary introspection starts to draw to an end, Auckland looks set to enter the post-Covid world with all of its well established charms still in place but complemented by some homegrown swagger, created under the unique conditions of the country's much-vaunted pandemic response.

Above: Auckland Museum's imposing neoclassical building holds a superlative collection of Māori and Pasifika artefacts.

Left: just one of the Māori treasures displayed on the museum's ground floor.

Previous spread: Waiheke Island.

TAIPEI, TAIWAŃ

GOOD TO KNOW

UTC +8hr

New Taiwan dollar

Mandarin, Taiwanese

International flights arrive at Taoyuan International Airport. Taipei Main Station is the railway hub for journeys all over Taiwan. Cruise ships dock at Keelung, 30km from Taipei.

• *Taiwan Literature: English Translation Series* University of California
• *A Culinary History of Taipei: Beyond Pork and Ponlai* Steven Crook & Katy Hui-wen Hung
• www.taipeitimes. com

You need a voracious appetite to do Taipei justice – and that's not just referring to its culinary gems, of which there are plenty. This is a city that deserves full-on exploration, a city where a wealth of ancient religious traditions sit alongside a progressive LGBT+ culture, and where hikers and cyclists can experience a series of micro-climates during the day and top-notch bars and restaurants in the evening. Taiwan's capital is an urban feast that will leave you satisfied.

MANY MONUMENTS, MULTIPLE GODS

Three hundred years in the making, modern Taipei is unhurried and vibrant, as comfortable with its mixed heritage of Chinese, Japanese, indigenous and Western influences as it is with the juxtaposition of old and new. Looking down from Taipei 101, the 508m-tall landmark that is the capital's highest building, contemporary constructions, modern facades, buildings in an eclectic Japanese-Western style, temples and parks all jostle for space – sometimes in the same district, such as in Da Dao Cheng. In many areas, growth has been visibly organic with old, sometimes improvised structures dispersed among much newer buildings. The sustainable practice of adaptive reuse is common – 19th-century railroad offices, tobacco factories and leper hospitals operate as museums and art villages to preserve history and better articulate cultural identity.

Temples are common in Taipei. The city is heir to the entire panoply of Chinese religions and traditions, from Buddhism to Taoism to Confu-cianism and an amorphous collection of deities worshipped as folk faith. Its temples reflect this diversity, with swallowtail-roofed beauties such as Longshan Temple and Nung Chan Monastery, an award-winning archi-tect's brainchild. Religious festivals take place throughout the year: loud, flamboyant affairs involving parades where spectators are welcome.

This inclusiveness extends into many other areas of city life. Taipei ranks high in global spatial inclusiveness indices for its relatively affordable housing and access to healthcare. And long before Taiwan became the first place in Asia to legalise same-sex marriage in 2019, Taipei enjoyed a reputation as Asia's most LGBT+-friendly city.

BIG THINGS IN SMALL PACKAGES
The island of Taiwan is relatively small

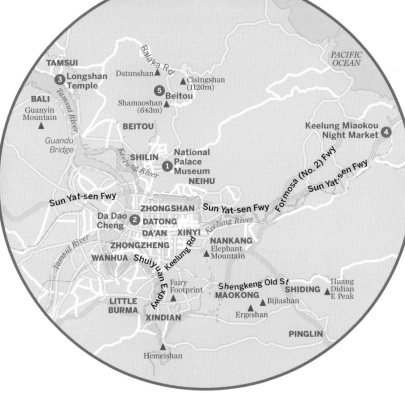

HIGHLIGHTS

1 National Palace Museum Huge, impressive collection of Chinese art spanning millennia.

2 Da Dao Cheng Tea, trade and architecture await in Taipei's oldest district.

3 Longshan Temple A treasure trove of folk faith and temple arts.

4 Keelung Miaokou Night Market A 200-stall food fest in a fishing port close to Taipei.

5 Beitou Hiking, hot springs and history in a mountainous suburb.

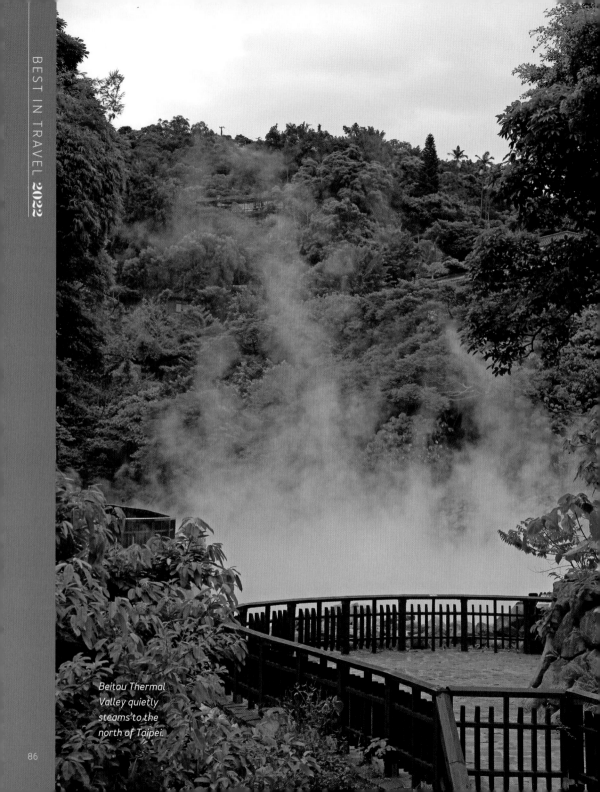

Beitou Thermal Valley quietly steams to the north of Taipei.

but that doesn't mean it's not naturally blessed and meteorologically diverse. The climate ranges from subtropical to subarctic, with vegetation zones from coastal to alpine. Two-thirds of its terrain is covered by mountains, with hundreds of peaks passing 3000m. Taipei itself is home to the beautiful Yangmingshan National Park, criss-crossed by hiking trails and cycling routes and dotted with 20 or so volcanoes, including Taipei's highest mountain, Qixing (1120m). The volcanoes are dormant but geothermal activity provides both a smell of rotten eggs and plenty of natural hot springs to soothe exercise-weary bodies. Yangmingshan is also famous for flowers: cherry blossoms in spring; hydrangea in early summer; silvergrass in autumn. And close to Yangmingshan, you can combine hiking and hot springs with history in the town of Beitou.

COME HUNGRY
The island's range of climates is ideal for growing everything from mangoes to cacao – Taiwanese fruits, in particular, are famously sweet and succulent. Consumers in the capital are discerning and obsessed with food safety and taste, so even at non-gourmet establishments, menus sometimes underscore 'terroir', some going as far as to name the farm and farmer.

Whether in a Michelin-starred restaurant where dishes present a chef-y spin on traditional comfort foods or at one of the city's multiple family-run outlets that rely on tried-and-tested, handed-down recipes, locally sourced raw materials are key to quality and happy diners.

In the celebrated night markets, many stalls have been specialising in the same dishes for generations. These markets were the products of less affluent times when people catered to the pedestrian traffic at temples, wharves and schools to make a living, helping peddle their wares by singing opera and performing magic tricks. Most of Taipei's night markets still retain their shopping and entertainment functions – buskers, phone-case sellers and ring-toss games are a common sight, making these nocturnal bazaars so much more than just an eating experience.

Another ingredient in the city's culinary mix is the large Southeast Asian community that calls Taipei home and which has helped to shape its dining scene: Vietnamese restaurants abound, serving excellent authentic *pho* and *banh mi*; Little Burma is a district where a small community of migrants from Thailand and Myanmar live and work.

Taipei's essence is perhaps best captured by the location of the new Taipei Performing Arts Center, next to a night market dating back to the 1900s. The sites have different uses, but both nourish and entertain in their individual ways – just like the city itself.

WHEN TO GO

JAN & FEB
The weeks bracketing the Lunar New Year are a great time to visit.

JUN-SEP
The hottest, typhoon-prone months are peak season for domestic travel.

OCT-DEC & MAR-MAY
Best time to visit with the heat gone and the chill yet to begin.

"The opening of the Taipei Performing Arts Center has been much anticipated. Architect Rem Koolhaas has responded to the informality of the neighbourhood with a cube and sphere."

CHANG WEIHSIU, ARCHITECT AND URBAN PLANNER

FREIBURG, GERMANY

With cobbled lanes, gabled townhouses, an ancient university and a skyline dominated by the spire of its cathedral, Freiburg checks all the boxes of cliched German quaintness. But don't be fooled. Beneath the pretty veneer you'll also discover one of the country's most youthful, relaxed and sustainable cities. With plenty of eco-accolades under its belt, the Black Forest's charismatic capital has a trick or two to teach many of us about living responsibly.

GOOD TO KNOW

UTC +1hr

Euro

German

EuroAirport Basel-Mulhouse-Freiburg is about 70km south of the city and connected by airport bus. Freiburg is also a stop on a major north-south rail corridor, with frequent connections to Baden-Baden and Basel.

• *In Free Fall* Juli Zeh
• *Eifelheim* Michael Flynn
• www.greencity. freiburg.de

PASSION FOR THE ENVIRONMENT

Freiburg has been a trailblazer of Germany's environmental movement since local activists prevented the construction of a nearby nuclear power plant in 1975. A smart public transportation system, twice as many bicycles as cars and lots of urban green spaces are only the basic ingredients in its cocktail of climate-friendly initiatives. Stir in a huge number of solar panels perched atop homes, public buildings, churches and even the football stadium to harness the region's abundant sunshine. Add several sustainable communities brimming with 'plus-energy' buildings that generate more power than they consume. And shake it up with a Green Industrial Park, Europe's largest solar research institute, and an architecturally striking new city hall that's the world's first with a zero-energy concept. All this environmental commitment contributes to Freiburg's enviably high quality of life, something that its 232,000 citizens are justifiably proud of and that makes this compact city such a captivating place to visit.

OLD TOWN TEMPTATIONS

Tap into Freiburg's relaxed vibe on an aimless meander through the Old Town, a joy thanks to its handsome looks, café-laced squares and absence of vehicle traffic – after WWII bombs reduced much of Freiburg to ashes, forward-looking city planners decided to rebuild the core in keeping with its medieval layout and to banish all cars.

A good place to start is at the mighty Gothic cathedral, Freiburger Münster, with its cloud-scraping spire, grimacing gargoyles and ornate entrance portal. Light filtering in through kaleidoscopic stained-glass windows creates a suitably tranquil atmosphere inside. Note the altar, a masterful work by Dürer protégé Hans Baldung Grien.

If the cathedral is Freiburg's spiritual heart, the busy farmers market

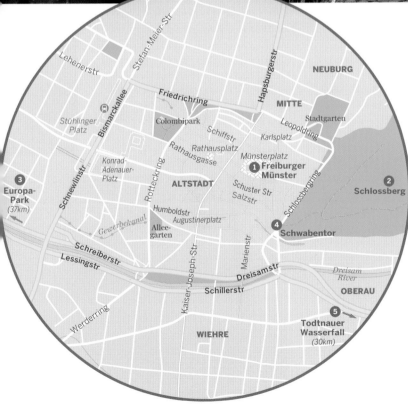

HIGHLIGHTS

1 **Freiburger Münster** Treasure-filled medieval cathedral with stellar views.

2 **Schlossberg** Local mountain reached on foot or by historic funicular.

3 **Europa-Park** Germany's largest theme park is a trip around Europe, one attraction at a time.

4 **Schwabentor** One of two surviving medieval gates, sporting a mural of St George slaying the dragon.

5 **Todtnauer Wasserfall** Splendid Black Forest waterfall that tumbles 97m over a rugged granite wall.

> ## "Freiburg is a lively, sunny, feel-good place and a great base for exploring the Black Forest. It's also very 'green', both physically and politically speaking."

SUSANNE FREGER
LOCAL TOUR GUIDE

on the surrounding square is its culinary soul. Every weekday morning it erupts in a feast of flavours and colours as local growers artfully arrange seasonal bounty, a tradition going back to the city's founding in 1120. In one section, smoke billows from a row of open grills where flames tickle the local cult snack Lange Rote – a 30cm-long grilled bratwurst tucked into a diminutive bun – to crispy perfection.

Sausage in hand, wander over to another famous landmark, the Historisches Kaufhaus, an arcaded 16th-century merchants' hall easily recognised by its blood-red facade and line-up of statues of Habsburg emperors.

Another of Freiburg's famous medieval vestiges is the network of Lilliputian canals known as Bächle. These paved gutters, paralleling the cobbled lanes, are fed by water diverted from the Dreisam River and were originally used to provide drinking water to livestock and to fight fires. Today, they're not only picturesque but provide an inge-nious natural cooling system on hot summer days. Feel free to dip in your toes but be careful not to step in – if you do, you must marry a Freiburger (or so the tradition dictates).

HEAD TO THE HILLS

If the thought of myths and legends sparks your imagination, head out of town and into the surrounding Black Forest, whose half-timbered villages look every inch the fairy-tale fantasy. Every bend in the road reveals a smile-inducing view, from cascading waterfalls to shimmering lakes, house-sized cuckoo clocks and famous vineyards to cafes serving kirsch-drenched Black Forest Gateau.

But it's the spirit-lifting hiking, biking and other low-impact, back-to-nature options that truly connect you with this land. A highlight is the Westweg, Germany's first long-distance hiking trail carved by

WHEN TO GO

JUN-AUG
Plenty of sunshine; optimal for outdoor activities from hiking to lake-swimming.

APR & MAY, SEP & OCT
Smaller crowds, spring bloom and autumn colours, plus moderate temperatures and rainfall.

NOV-MAR
Coldest months with short days; skiing in the Black Forest January to March.

intrepid pioneers over a century ago. The 285-kilometre route dips through valleys and forests, past panoramic peaks and lakes steeped in legend. A true classic, but not for the unfit.

Freiburg's dedication to nature, conservation and sustainability extends to the Black Forest as well. Along with 28 rural communities, the city forms part of the Black Forest Biosphere Reserve, designated by Unesco in 2017, a wonderfully eclectic landscape with a climate that ranges from subalpine to near-Mediterranean. Butterflies flutter and endangered lynx lurk among large swathes of mixed forest, moors, rivers and lakes, while ancient cattle breeds graze on so-called 'Allmend' pastures, known for their stunning biodiversity. With only a few such pastures still existing in Germany, their preservation is a key goal of a reserve that's being developed as a model for the wider, sustainable coexistence of nature, people and commerce.

Above: kick off your city tour at Freiburger Münster, with its High Altar by Hans Baldung Grien.

Left: walk the long-distance Westweg through the beautiful Black Forest.

Previous spread: the city has a network of cobbled lanes and mini canals.

ATLANTA, USA

GOOD TO KNOW

UTC -5hr

US dollar

English

Hartsfield-Jackson Atlanta International Airport has flights from around the US and the world. The city is also serviced by Amtrak.

• *Where the Crawdads Sing* Delia Owens
. *An American Marriage* Tayari Jones
. www.atlanta magazine.com

Nicknamed 'Hotlanta' for its contemporary energy and sweltering summers, Atlanta is a thriving, shining cultural jewel in the heart of the American South. A city that has passion and activism in its soul – the birthplace of Martin Luther King Jr was a major battleground state during the United States' 2020 presidential election – is also home to an invigorated arts scene and cutting-edge sustainability initiatives. Atlanta is hotter, and cooler, than ever.

AN ATLANTA RENAISSANCE

Located in northwestern Georgia, Atlanta is the peach state's largest city and also its most dynamic, recently re-emerging as a hotbed of artistic creativity, cultural inspiration and urban magnetism.

Musically, this place has long been home to some of the greatest, from Ray Charles, Gladys Knight, Usher, Jermaine Dupri and Outkast to 21 Savage, Childish Gambino, Killer Mike and Gucci Mane. Writers are also turning to Atlanta as a setting for their works, such as Delia Owens' *Where the Crawdads Sing* and Tayari Jones' *An American Marriage* – both bestselling contemporary novels based in the city. Major film and television studios (CNN, Turner Broadcasting and Tyler Perry) are Atlanta-based and bring exciting new projects, aspiring actors and fresh journalists to the city in droves, while hit shows *The Walking Dead*, *Stranger Things* and, unsurprisingly, *Atlanta* call 'The Big Peach' home.

And at community level, art projects like Living Walls, ABV, OuterSpace, Dashboard and Notch 8 are reviving an avant-garde spirit with incredible art installations and expansive murals that enliven the city's public spaces.

In addition to this creative renaissance, a multitude of new small, family- and Black-owned businesses provide straight-to-the source access to Atlanta's diverse, local communities: London Grant Co, a luscious eco-luxe skincare brand; Brave + Kind Bookshop; and Slutty Vegan, a food hot-spot which doubles as a meeting point for activists like Fair Fight, a non-profit founded by powerhouse local politician Stacey Abrams.

Atlanta's current political dynamism and cultural vibrancy are reflected in world class institutions, old and new, such as the King Center, the National Center for Civil and Human Rights and the High Museum of Art, which dedicate themselves to inclusivity and diversity in their

CENTER FOR CIVIL AND HUMAN RIGHTS

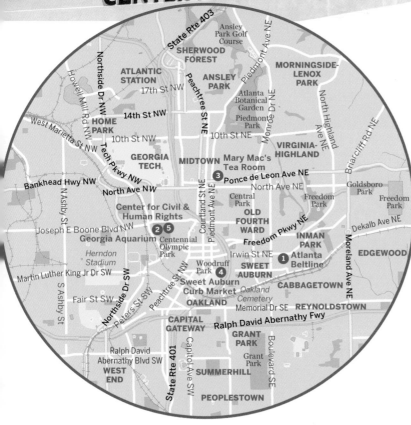

State Rte 403
Ansley Park Golf Course
SHERWOOD FOREST
Northside Dr NW
ATLANTIC STATION
17th St NW
ANSLEY PARK
Peachtree St NE
Piedmont Ave NE
MORNINGSIDE-LENOX PARK
North Highland Ave NE
Atlanta Botanical Garden
Monroe Dr NE
14th St NW
Howell Mill Rd NW
West Marietta St NW
HOME PARK
Tech Pkwy NW
10th St NW
Piedmont Park
10th St NE
Briarcliff Rd NE
GEORGIA TECH
MIDTOWN
Mary Mac's Tea Room
VIRGINIA-HIGHLAND
Bankhead Hwy NW
N Ashby St
North Ave NW
❸ Ponce de Leon Ave NE
Courtland St NE
Piedmont Ave NE
North Ave NE
Goldsboro Park
Central Park
Freedom Park
Freedom Park
Joseph E Boone Blvd NW
Center for Civil & Human Rights
OLD FOURTH WARD
Freedom Pkwy NE
Dekalb Ave NE
❷❺ Georgia Aquarium
Centennial Olympic Park
INMAN PARK
EDGEWOOD
Martin Luther King Jr Dr SW
Herndon Stadium
Irwin St NE
❶ Atlanta Beltline
Moreland Ave NE
Fair St SW
S Ashby St
Peachtree St NW
Woodruff Park ❹
SWEET AUBURN
CABBAGETOWN
Northside Dr SW
Peters St SW
Sweet Auburn Curb Market
Oakland Cemetery
OAKLAND
Memorial Dr SE
REYNOLDSTOWN
CAPITAL GATEWAY
Ralph David Abernathy Fwy
Capitol Ave SW
Ralph David Abernathy Blvd SW
State Rte 401
GRANT PARK
Grant Park
Boulevard SE
WEST END
SUMMERHILL
PEOPLESTOWN

HIGHLIGHTS

❶ **The Beltline** 50km of former railroad tracks connect neighbourhoods to green spaces and parks.

❷ **Georgia Aquarium** The largest aquarium in the US, with 500 species.

❸ **Mary Mac's Tea Room** 'Atlanta's Dining Room' serves classic homemade Southern cuisine.

❹ **Sweet Auburn Curb Market** Busy market and historical landmark.

❺ **National Center for Civil and Human Rights** Vast, fascinating, moving museum.

Hip-hop duo El-P and Atlanta-based Killer Mike, aka Run the Jewels, perform at the city's Tabernacle concert hall.

permanent and visiting collections. Family-friendly staples like the Georgia Aquarium, the Children's Museum of Atlanta, the Coca-Cola Museum, Legoland and a new $1.5 billion stadium round out the city's attractions.

Along with the diversity of Atlanta's sights comes a demographic diversity too. Around 58% of residents are Black and the city has a thriving LGBT+ community, meaning that what for many places is a dream of diversity and representation across all industries, is a full-on reality in Atlanta, happening here today. Visitors of all ages, genders, races, nationalities and sexual orientations are welcomed with open arms and, of course, some good old-fashioned Southern hospitality.

THE CITY IN A FOREST

In addition to its many charms, Atlanta is also surfing the cutting edge of the sustainability wave. The city offers a one-of-a-kind skyline and topography due to the fact that a whopping 48% of the urban area is covered in trees. A non-profit organisation famous for its love of greenery and passion for protecting it, Trees Atlanta partners daily with municipal officials to doggedly protect the city's stunning canopy. In 2020, the group enacted the landmark One Million Trees Initiative, 'a collaboration of 10 local non-profits and 10 metro Atlanta cities to plant and conserve 1,000,000 trees in 10 years'. To help with the scheme, visitors and locals are welcome to volunteer, donate or gift a tree to the city.

Atlanta is also expanding its urban infrastructure to reduce carbon emissions via The Beltline, plus expanded pedestrian and biking paths and carpooling initiatives. The city ranks fifth nationwide in ENERGY STAR-certified buildings engineered to generate fewer greenhouse gas emissions than average – 287 green buildings eliminate 275,000 units of emissions annually, with energy-cost savings of $54.1 million. Atlanta's population is expected to grow by three million in the next two decades, thanks to both an influx of new residents drawn to its economic opportunities, warm climate and affordable housing, and the dispersed African American southerners returning home to engage with the new cultural landscape. Helping the city develop sustainably will be a key challenge, but Atlanta seems on track to achieve the right balance between growth and environmental protection. Perhaps more-so than at any other time in its history, local legend Ray Charles' sweet serenade rings true: 'Georgia, Georgia...my sweet Georgia... the road leads back to you.'

WHEN TO GO

MAR-MAY, SEPT & OCT
Spring is rainy but pleasantly warm; autumn is sunny, cool and dry.

NOV-FEB
Atlanta's winters are usually dry, snow-free and mild.

JULY & AUG
Summer is very hot and humid with frequent thunderstorms.

"Atlanta's unique appeal is getting stronger. My top choices? Picnics in Piedmont Park, The Beltline, dinners at 9 Mile Station and the South African jerky from Biltong Bar."

LINDSEY EPPERLY
CEO, EPPERLY TRAVEL

LAGOS,
NIGERIA

05

GOOD TO KNOW

UTC +1hr

Naira

English, Pidgin, Hausa, Yoruba, Igbo, Edo, Efik

Murtala Muhammed International Airport (MMA1) is the main gateway to Nigeria and is roughly 10km north of Lagos Island. There are no airport buses into the city; take a taxi.

• *Easy Motion Tourist* Leye Adenle
• *Blackass* A. Igoni Barrett
• *Everything Good Will Come* Sefi Atta

With champagne-soaked beach parties, a celebrated Afrobeat music scene and a world-class Fashion Week, Lagos is a city that demands attention. This fervid, oil-rich metropolis on Nigeria's southwest coast is bursting with creativity although, for many of its 22 million inhabitants, Lagos is not without its challenges. In a world of increasing homogeneity, the unique excitement of Lagos – or 'Las Gidi' as it's nicknamed (translation: 'real Lagos') – will leave your head spinning in the best possible way.

RISE OF A MEGACITY

It's hard to believe that Africa's third biggest city was once a sleepy Yoruba fishing village set on a system of lagoons. When the Portuguese arrived they named the area Lagos ('lakes' in Portuguese), and under British rule it became the centre of Nigerian politics, commerce and entertainment, growing exponentially, attracting people from all corners of the country and becoming the megacity that it is today. Until 1991 it was Nigeria's capital, and while these days the federal government is found in Abuja, the country's centre of gravity remains fixed on Lagos.

For a time the city had a bad reputation, but in the last couple of decades it has cleaned up its act and flourished as a commercial and cultural powerhouse that exports films, music and fashion to the rest of Africa and beyond. Though Lagos' importance within Nigeria and the continent keeps growing, the wider world is yet to catch on to a city that is often undervalued as a destination.

LAGOS FOR VISITORS

For the traveller there are three main areas to explore. First up is Lagos Island, the original heart of the city. Take a ride along Bámgbósé St here, past outdoor markets piled with fruit, live chickens and women in brightly coloured dresses selling smoked fish. At the end of the street you'll find an example of the old houses built by formerly enslaved people and their descendants who returned to Lagos from Brazil in the 19th century. These buildings represent a strong cultural connection to Brazil, where the deities of the Candomblé religion there still have Yoruba-language names.

The second area, Ikeja, is close to the main airport and is a well-planned residential district with hotels and music venues such as the famous Fela Kuti's Afrika Shrine.

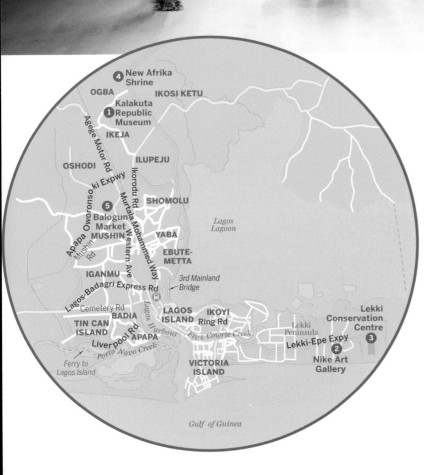

HIGHLIGHTS

1 **Kalakuta Republic Museum** Fela Kuti's former home, preserved as it was when he lived there.

2 **Nike Art Gallery** Run by artist Nike Okundaye and filled with modern and traditional Nigerian arts.

3 **Lekki Conservation Centre** Spot monkeys, crocs and wetland birds from canopy walkways.

4 **New Afrika Shrine** Catch shows by Fela's talented sons Femi and Seun.

5 **Balogun Market** A maze of clothes and fabrics from across West Africa.

> "Lagos sucked me in. I had no choice. I thought 'Oh my god, I can't go back!' The energy, the rawness — it's a blank canvas with 22 million people."

HUNDERSON SABBAT
MANAGER, ALARA CONCEPT STORE

Finally, upmarket Victoria Island is home to embassies, art galleries, fancy restaurants and exclusive beaches where horses gallop, the air throbs with party music and the aroma of *suya* (fiery beef skewers) mingles with the sea breeze.

CONSTANT CREATIVITY

With a population estimated at around 22 million, the city has a diversity and energy that consistently produces fresh cultural innovations. Lagos' list of pioneers include the legendary singer Fela Kuti, the inventor of Afrobeat, in which he mixed funk and Latin rhythms with highlife, a very danceable type of West African popular music that plays traditional Ghanaian songs using Western instruments.

Lagos is also home to Nollywood, the third-largest film industry in the world, which churns out movies from high-end slick flicks to low-budget B-movies. This rough-and-ready innovative spirit is also reflected in works by artists such as Dotun Popoola, who has gained international recognition by fashioning beautiful sculptures from scrap metal.

To get the most out of this sometimes intimidating metropolis, the key is to just dive in, enjoying and contributing to a local economy which has much to offer in terms of live music, food and art galleries. Plan a trip to coincide with the Aké Arts and Books Festival, which draws an exciting, international crowd,

WHEN TO GO

NOV-FEB
Best time to arrive is in the dry high season: humidity decreases and the harmattan blows in (Dec-Jan). Mid-October is Felebration time in Lagos, a celebration of Fela Kuti.

MAR & OCT
The shoulder season; the rains begin in March.

APR-SEP
The low season sees heavy rainfall and journeys can be slow outside of the city.

or with ART X Lagos, West Africa's first international art fair run by one of the many diasporans who have returned to inject expertise and energy into the city. Check out Kalakuta Republic Museum, where Kuti's former home has been preserved in its original form and displays everything from family photos to his trademark underpants. And escape the city to visit the Lekki Conservation Centre, a nature reserve that takes you back to pre-industrial Lagos.

The Covid-19 pandemic might have broken the city's stride briefly, but life is back to normal and Lagos' growth shows no signs of slowing, with projects in the pipeline such as an exhibition gallery at the JK Randle Centre for Yoruba Culture and History. In an era of Instagrammed global over-tourism, Lagos is an adventurous destination that doesn't commodify itself to lure tourists. It exists on its own terms, creating an authenticity that makes it a perfect city to head to in 2022.

Above: mangrove forest is protected at Lekki Conservation Centre.

Left: a classic Nigerian dish of jollof rice, chicken and fried plantain.

Previous spread: Arise Fashion Week in December is a highlight of Lagos' calendar.

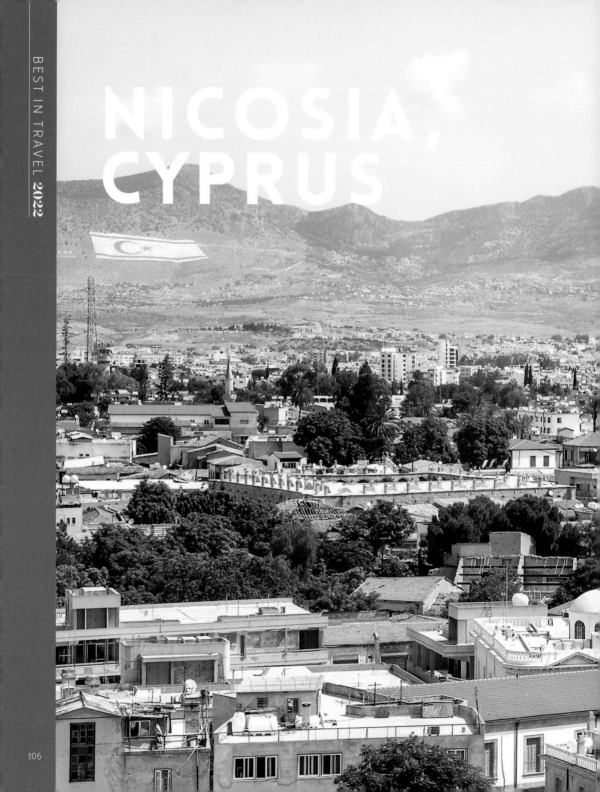

NICOSIA, CYPRUS

GOOD TO KNOW

UTC +2hr

Euro (south), Turkish lira (north)

Greek (south), Turkish (north)

The main airports are in Larnaka (Larnaca) and Pafos (Paphos) in the south, linked by airport shuttle bus (45min from Larnaka; 2hr from Pafos) to Nicosia.

• *Journey into Cyprus* Colin Thubron
• *Gregory and Other Stories* Panos Ioannides
• www.cyprus-mail. com

The sun-scorched city of Nicosia (Lefkosia) in Cyprus has been split by a UN-patrolled buffer zone since 1974, its Greek and Turkish halves living largely separate lives. But while the pandemic saw borders elsewhere around the world closing, the reaction here was the emergence of cross-community cultural projects, meaning an exploration of the world's only remaining divided capital and its curious mash-up of Mediterranean cultures has never been so compelling.

CONTEMPLATING THE BIG PICTURE
Culturally European yet geographically Middle Eastern, a rich and flamboyant, no-holds-barred urban cocktail of Greek, Turkish, Muslim and Christian influences. That's Nicosia. But before diving into Cyprus' bustling split capital, take time to bike and hike north of town to Mount Pentadaktylos (Beşparmak in Turkish) to contemplate the big picture. This particular picture is the size of 40 football pitches, a giant red-on-white star and crescent flag, created with coloured stones on the hillside here and representing the breakaway Turkish Republic of Northern Cyprus (TRNA) that has covered the northern part of the island since 1983 (but is only recognised by Turkey).

Back in Nicosia, no single city sight is so hard to ignore as the flag (it's visible from numerous spots) or is such a powerful reminder of the centuries of relentless conflict that have shaped this intriguing destination.

CROSSING THE GREEN LINE
The Green Line, the UN buffer zone, has sliced through Nicosia since the Turkish invasion in 1974. To walk across it is to confront the island's complex history and experience the physical division between the Republic of Cyprus in the south and the TRNA in the north. Shops, museums, art galleries, swanky squares, café terraces belting out *bouzouki* blues and candlelit churches adorned with Byzantine icons in the south give way to a time-warp of labyrinthine bazaars, Gothic mosques, grand Ottoman caravanserai and decaying townhouses in North Nicosia (Lefkoşa in Turkish). Above all, to cross this 'Green Line' – so-called after a simple line drawn on a military map in green pen by the British to define Greek and Turkish areas in 1963 – is to encounter Nicosia's two dramatically different yet deeply entwined communities: the majority of Greek Cypriots and Turkish Cypriots these days perceive themselves as Cypriot first, Greek or Turkish second.

The caravanserai or inn of Büyük Han.

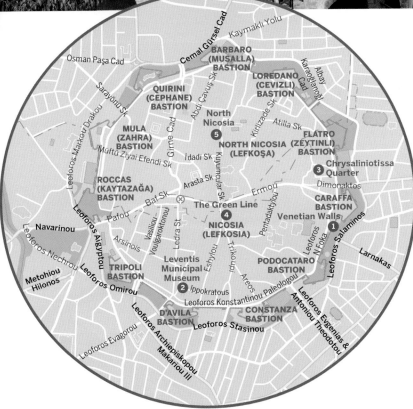

HIGHLIGHTS

1 **Venetian Walls** Explore snowflake-shaped 16th-century fortifications.

2 **Leventis Municipal Museum** Untangle Nicosia's complex, fascinating past.

3 **Chrysaliniotissa Quarter** Revitalised district with flower-fringed cottages and restored townhouses.

4 **The Green Line** Walk the line bisecting Europe's last divided capital.

5 **North Nicosia** Time-travel through Gothic arches at a stunning cathedral-turned-mosque and Ottoman Büyük Han.

Take a break from Nicosia's sights to kick back with a cup of strong local coffee poured from a traditional *mbriki*.

In reality, the Green Line is not a line at all but an eerie no-man's-land of derelict houses, overgrown gardens, bullet-pocked public buildings and sandbag barriers, interspersed with UN checkpoints through which locals and tourists pass. Exploring the ancient tangle of streets tucked within city walls built by Venetian rulers to ward off Ottoman invaders is a lesson in human resilience. Decades of failed peace talks and living in de facto separation, fused with the Covid-19 pandemic that closed borders and devastated tourism, has forged a new determination at community level among the Cypriots to promote peace through culture on both sides of the north-south divide.

CELEBRATING SHARED HERITAGE

Restoring architectural monuments – Ottoman-era drinking fountains, historic churches and mosques – using bi-communal teams of archaeologists, engineers and architects has been the community-building focus of the EU-funded Technical Committee on Cultural Heritage for several years. Its #oursharedheritage hashtag shines light on pristine new treasures awaiting visitors in 2022: take an urban stroll through time, from the ancient city-kingdom of Ledra to the politically charged present.

When strict pandemic lockdown measures closed checkpoint crossings – controversially blocking free movement for the first time since their historic opening in 2003 – Cypriots joined together either side of the Line's barbed-wire fences to sing in unison. Covid-19 also spawned United by Sound, a collaborative-arts project based at Nicosia's groundbreaking House for Cooperation community centre in the demilitarised buffer zone. Striving to connect Cypriot communities and encourage dialogue through music, it joined 40 musicians online from homes all over the island in summer 2020 to record *The Time is Ripe*, a catchy track with lyrics in English, Greek and Turkish. Not only was this song by the so-called Island Seeds a heart-bursting call to action to 'bring our voice together', 'love our neighbours' and 'live in peace', the ethnically mixed lineup of artists – several of Palestinian, Lebanese or Armenian descent – was a pertinent reflection of modern-day Cyprus' diversity. The ongoing stream of other music events backed by the House for Cooperation, including rooftop concerts by local musicians at the Home Café and the annual Buffer Fringe performing-arts festival, are all equally worthy reasons to linger over a glass of ice-cold ouzo and traditional meze plates on a café terrace in Nicosia in 2022, adding your own voice to these encouraging cross-communal enterprises.

WHEN TO GO

APR-JUN, SEP & OCT
Pleasantly warm days, with occasional rain showers, entice the largest tourist crowds.

JUL & AUG
Temperatures soar; locals leg it to the coast.

NOV-MAR
Cold evenings and sometimes rainy days.

"In the middle of Nicosia's buffer zone, the artistic and cultural programmes at our unique community centre work hard to promote peace, dialogue and coexistence."

HAYRIYE RÜZGAR
HOME FOR COOPERATION, NICOSIA

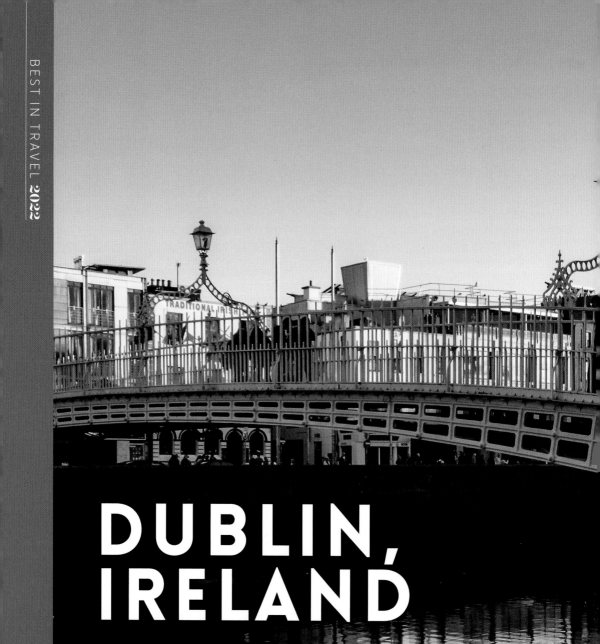

DUBLIN, IRELAND

© PREVIOUS PAGE: JOSE ANTONIO MACIEL | GETTY IMAGES, ABOVE: ANDREW MONTGOMERY | LONELY PLANET

GOOD TO KNOW

UTC

Euro

English, Irish

Dublin is well
connected thanks
to its international
airport; Dublin Port
(6km from the city
centre) has ferries
from Wales, England,
France and the Isle
of Man.

• *Ulysses* James Joyce
• *Love* Roddy Doyle
• www.lovindublin.
com

On 16 June 1904 Leopold Bloom took a stroll around Dublin. Leopold might have been a fictional character, the protagonist of modernist novel *Ulysses* by James Joyce that was published in full in 1922, but the real city he walked around on his Irish odyssey, with its Georgian squares, traditional pubs and warm people, is still there a century on. And its long established highlights are now complemented by new layers of community and diversity that add to the capital's contemporary appeal.

DUBLIN, FAIR CITY

Split by the River Liffey and bordered north and south by two canals – true Dubliners, like Bloom, are said to be born between them – the capital's core is as compact and easy to navigate now as it was a hundred years ago. The Southside is where you find museums, elegant squares, famous Trinity College with the *Book of Kells*, shop-filled Grafton St – and the Guinness Storehouse, which has been brewing the black stuff since 1759. Across the Liffey, the North-side has emerged as an area of cool microbreweries and cutting-edge restaurants, as well as being home to the James Joyce Centre, some of the capital's most striking – the Four Courts – and historically important – the General Post Office – buildings, and the massive, easy-to-lose-yourself-in Phoenix Park.

A DIVERSE CITY

Across the city, north and south, you'll find another of Dublin's long-established attractions, its people. Characters that Bloom could have met on his summer perambulation are still very much in evidence, retaining a spirit which ensures that despite a world-changing pandemic, Dublin remains one of Europe's most down-to-earth and friendly cities.

There's also a new aspect to Dublin's traditional population, a more international, cosmopolitan mix that's helping to create big changes in the city. A youthful, highly educated population and accompanying social scene added to a healthy influx of non-nationals drawn to one of Europe's tech hubs go some way to explaining Dublin's contemporary liberal dynamism. This is the capital of the first country to introduce gay marriage through the ballot box in 2015, and where a Citizens' Assembly discusses and reports on major issues such as abortion and climate change to a parliament that is obliged to respond.

HIGHLIGHTS

1 **Trinity College** Historic city-centre campus, home to the ancient *Book of Kells* and the Old Library.

2 **National Gallery** Take in a Caravaggio and works by Jack B. Yeats, brother of poet William Butler.

3 **Kilmainham Gaol** Former prison, the execution site of many of the 1916 Easter Rising leaders.

4 **Guinness Storehouse** Savour a 'pint of plain' with panoramic views.

5 **Little Museum of Dublin** Award-winning museum telling the story of Dublin.

"Joyce famously said 'When I die Dublin will be written in my heart' and visiting the city you quickly realise that a love of storytelling runs deep in Dublin's DNA."

LIZ HALPIN
HEAD OF DUBLIN REGION, FÁILTE IRELAND

THE FUTURE HAS TWO WHEELS

As Leopold Bloom demonstrated, Dublin is a highly walkable city, but in recent years there's also been a trend towards cycling, a process that accelerated during the pandemic lockdown. Many Dubliners took to bike riding as a mode of transport, exercise and a way to escape being stuck indoors. Eco-friendly bike schemes saw pop-up segregated cycle routes around the city which proved so popular that many became permanent. Biking stations make renting two wheels easy, and half of them are hybrid electric in case your legs get a bit wobbly. It's now possible to pedal 10km of attractive coastline between Sandymount strand, where Bloom famously ogled girls from the rocks, to Sandycove tower, featured in the book's opening chapter and site of the James Joyce Museum & Tower. A few minutes from the latter is the Forty Foot, a bracing seawater pool in which one of the characters in *Ulysses* bathes. Once the preserve of men, the pool is now open to everyone brave enough to take the plunge. And alongside cycling initiatives, car-parking spaces have been repurposed into dining areas, creating a wonderful village-like feel in parts of the capital.

ETHICAL TOURISM

Bloom would have been happy to see that Sweny's pharmacy on Lincoln Place has changed little since he called in on that June day and, like he did, you can still come here to

WHEN TO GO

MAY-SEPT
Busiest time of year.
Don't trust the word
'summer' – rain and
chilly temperatures
are just as likely as sun
and warmth.

MAR-APR & OCT-NOV
Easter marks the start
of the visitor season
but sees fewer
crowds. Numbers
wane in October and
November too.

DEC-FEB
Erratic weather –
but you can warm
yourself with a hot
toddy among locals in
a traditional pub.

buy its lemon-scented soap. Similar artisan products, crafts and foods now crop up in a wealth of independent shops that have flourished in the same Southside neighbourhood since the pandemic, creating a renewed sense of community. The streets here that are home to some of the city's top free attractions featured in the novel (the National Gallery, the National Museum of Ireland, the National Library) are also included in a plan to pedestrianise parts of the area. Shopping local and secondhand has been another positive outcome of Covid-19 – on Camden St, across St Stephen's Green from Sweny's, you'll find a trove of charity shops selling pre-loved clothes and books (see if you can find a copy of *Ulysses*), while a stroll west in Dublin's medieval quarter, Francis St is renowned for its antiques. Modern Dublin still has all the appeal of the city in Joyce's day plus a host of compelling contemporary reasons to visit now. Bring comfortable shoes – there's lots to discover.

Above: rent a bike and pedal north of Dublin's centre to dip a toe (or more) in the bracing waters of Forty Foot seawater pool.

Left: immortalised in Marjorie Fitzgibbon's North Earl St statue, James Joyce is a Dublin icon.

Previous spread: the Liffey flows past the Four Courts and Custom House building.

MÉRIDA, MEXICO

GOOD TO KNOW

UTC -5hr

Mexican peso

Spanish, Maya, English

Most international flights to Mérida make connections through Mexico City. Alternatively, some international airlines fly directly into Cancún where you can rent a car for the 300km drive to Mérida.

• *Incidents of Travel in Yucatán* John Lloyd Stephens
• *The Maya* Michael D Coe
• www.theyucatan times.com

Itching to tap into the pulse of the Yucatán Peninsula? Say adiós to party central Cancún and hightail it to state capital Mérida, the heart of this sultry corner of southeast Mexico. History, culture and nature come alive in this spirited region as you explore ancient Maya ruins, striking colonial buildings and mysterious cenotes. As for the thriving culinary move-ment, let's just say Mérida has well earned its cred as one of Mexico's finest food destinations.

CYCLING THROUGH HISTORY

Mérida has stood at the forefront of the Yucatán's cultural scene since the Spanish conquest 500 years ago, and the so-called White City only seems to be growing in popularity as more and more travellers look to soak up the region's rich heritage.

Most of the action unfolds around Mérida's busy historic centre, where new art galleries, hip fan-cooled cantinas, innovative restaurants and a slew of museums and live events are producing an increasingly vibrant downtown atmosphere. Visitors spend most of their time between this colonial centre and the quieter Paseo de Montejo, a parade of aris-tocratic mansions, trendy sidewalk cafes and iconic monuments, named after one of the city's founders. Because the tree-lined *paseo* is one of Mérida's longest and most beauti-ful avenues, it has become a popular weekend cycling route as the city steps up its support for sustainable transportation – in the ongoing effort to make Mérida more bicycle-friendly, Paseo de Montejo is closed to cars on Sunday mornings. And in addition to an ever-expanding bike-lane network, the local government now offers subsidies on new bicycle purchases.

Bikes are ideal for reaching many sights beyond the city as well, such as refreshingly cool cenotes (natural swimming pools created by limestone sinkholes) and lovely old haciendas where *henequen* (a type of agave) was farmed. And if you can't live without the beach, you can head out to the nearby coastal town of Progreso (35km north of downtown). Keep in mind, though, that Mérida gets downright hot and muggy from April to October, so plan your pedaling for the early morning or late afternoon.

MEET THE MAYA

Maya culture serves as a constant reminder of the region's wondrous past, and that important influence

Mayan ruins at Uxmal, south of Mérida.

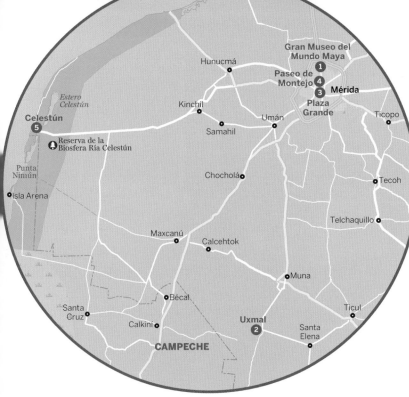

HIGHLIGHTS

1 **Gran Museo del Mundo Maya** Magnificent museum celebrating Maya culture.

2 **Uxmal** Sophisticated Maya ruins without the crowds of Chichén Itzá.

3 **Plaza Grande** Mérida's pretty, lively main square offers live events, contemporary art and a cathedral as old as the city itself.

4 **Paseo de Montejo** Broad avenue lined with stately old mansions and pavement cafes.

5 **Celestún** Spot birds in the reserve near this sleepy, searing-hot village.

Mérida is a gourmand's heaven, with a host of places to taste-test the local cuisine.

very much lives on in Mérida today. To begin your exploration of this fascinating culture, a must-visit is the Gran Museo del Mundo Maya, a world-class museum in the north of the city housing over a thousand remarkably intact artefacts. It's an essential stop to brush up on all things Maya before hitting the area's ruins such as Chichén Itzá, Uxmal and Dzibilchaltún, which showcase the Maya's mind-blowing contributions to architecture, mathematics, astronomy and art. And those ancient, refreshing cenotes visitors take a dip in these days? They were believed by the Maya to be sacred entrances to the underworld – some were even used for human sacrifices.

To delve further into Maya culture, Mérida-based fair trade cooperative Alianza Peninsular para el Turismo Comunitario offers tours to seldom-visited villages with activities such as kayaking, birdwatching and traditional crafts demonstrations. Not only does this directly support local Maya economies but it also allows you to have a more personal experience with the people living in the communities.

Back in the city, market stalls and restaurants regularly use pre-Hispanic ingredients such as chaya (Mexican spinach), cacao and annatto-seed spice to create one-of-a-kind Yucatecan dishes.

EAT YOUR WAY THROUGH MÉRIDA
Which brings us to Mérida's current status as a cool culinary destination. The exquisite regional cuisine, coupled with an eclectic offering of international fare, has put the city on the map as one of the best places to eat in all of Mexico. Drawing on Maya, Caribbean, European and Middle Eastern influences, food is a tremendous source of pride across the peninsula and it shows in the capital's family-run restaurants, busy markets and ubiquitous street stalls, where classics such as panuchos (fried tortillas stuffed with refried beans) and sopa de lima (lime soup with shredded turkey or chicken) are served with gusto.

Locals rave about the castakan tortas (crispy pork belly sandwich) at Wayan'e as well as the outstanding contemporary Yucatecan cuisine at Manjar Blanco. For memorable market eats, Santa Ana Market's hole-in-the-wall La Socorrito has been perfecting the art of cochinita pibil (achiote-rubbed, slow-cooked pork) for more than six decades, while for tasty vegan fare trendsetting Lo Que Hay serves delectable three-course meals in the serene courtyard of Hotel Medio Mundo. The city is also seeing a growing number of foreign chefs taking their talents to Mérida – and who can blame them for wanting to set up shop in one of the sweetest colonial capitals in all of Mexico.

WHEN TO GO

NOV-FEB
Best time to visit, with pleasantly cool and mostly dry weather.

MAR-MAY
Average temperatures are high and there's a chance of rain.

JUN-OCT
Very hot, rainy and humid.

> "A Maya market vendor best captured the essence of Mérida. I was always in a hurry and she told me. 'Being in a hurry is not elegant'."

NELSON LAPREBENDERE
OWNER, HOTEL MEDIO MUNDO

09

FLORENCE, ITALY

GOOD TO KNOW

UTC +1hr

Euro

Italian

Florence Airport
is linked by tram
and shuttle bus to
the centre; Pisa
International Airport
is close by, with trains
from the city to
Florence's Stazione
Santa Maria Novella.

• *House of Secrets*
Allison Levy
• *Florentine: The True
Cuisine of Florence*
Emiko Davies
• www.theflorentine.
net

Home of the Renaissance and some of the world's finest art and architecture, Florence requires no introduction. From fashionable stop on every Grand Tour in the 18th century to modern mass tourism destination, Italy's famously over-crowded *città d'arte* (art city) is no stranger to those after some dolce vita. But when the global pandemic emptied it of visitors and income, the Tuscan capital had to rethink its future, forging an exciting new art journey in the process.

NATURALLY BRILLIANT – AND BUSY
Hotbed of exceptional craftsmanship and creativity since medieval times, the city of Florence (Firenze in Italian) has been blessed with artistic brilliance since birth. From Giotto's bell tower and Brunelleschi's magnificent burnt-red dome crowning the cathedral to the awe-inspiring sweep of Piazza della Signoria where sinful Botticelli canvases went up in flames on Savonarola's chilling Bonfire of the Vanities in 1497 and Michelangelo's *David* originally stood (today tucked away for safekeeping in its own purpose-built gallery, Galleria dell'Accademia), the historic heart of Florence heaves with iconic masterpieces admired the world over – and with those who want to see them. Indeed, prior to Covid-19, together with Venice and Rome the Tuscan capital typically contributed one-third of Italy's tourism income. In 2019 a record 16 million tourists packed out the photogenic web of historic streets and squares in its tiny Centro Storico, waiting for hours to snap selfies in the blockbuster Uffizi gallery, haggling over knock-off Gucci bags with street hawkers, and returning home bearing a pair of souvenir boxer shorts emblazoned with David's packet from an ancient city bearing an increasingly uncanny likeness to a theme park. But then Covid-19 brought over-touristed Florence to an apocalyptic standstill.

GRASSROOTS REBOOT
A dynamic community of modern-day artisans and creatives is still the lifeblood of the city – just as they were in 13th- and 14th-century Florence when merchant and craft guilds ruled the roost. Then, cobblers made leather shoes in *botteghe* (workshops) on Via del Calzaiuoli; dyers and tanners clustered around Via dei Conciatori and Corso dei Tintori; and jewellers crafted gold and silver to dazzling effect in ateliers

HIGHLIGHTS

1 **Galleria degli Uffizi** Marvel at masterpieces by Botticelli, Michelangelo, Da Vinci, Giotto and Raphael.

2 **The Duomo** Climb the frescoed cupola to enjoy a glorious city panorama.

3 **Trattoria Mario** Sink your teeth into a bloody-blue T-bone steak at this legendary restaurant.

4 **Medici Chapels** Haunting tomb sculptures made by Michelangelo himself.

5 **Caffè Rivoire** Drink in café culture at this historic spot in monumental Piazza della Signoria.

> ## "Florence has a great legacy of the past that is forever present and, now more than ever, inspires constant discovery of the handmade and heartfelt."
>
> BETTY SOLDI
> FLORENTINE CALLIGRAPHER, DESIGNER & CREATIVE THINKER

perched high above the River Arno on the medieval stone bridge of Ponte Vecchio. Now, rebooting this incredible grassroots artistic heritage is at the core of new initiatives to decentralise tourism (in other words, tempt visitors away from the overcrowded bijou gem that is the diminutive historic centre) and make it more sustainable and community-driven. Schemes include walking tours of fountains, newsstand street art and secret stargazing spots all over the city; behind-the-scenes visits to art studios; and guided hikes in the Bellosguardo hills culminating at a crafts centre in the Oltrarno neighbourhood where 20 artists and artisans share their ancient know-how and modern creativity in a 19th-century convent. Part of the world-famous art collection at the Galleria degli Uffizi has boldly moved to other venues in Florence and Tuscany in a bid to disperse the museum's crowds and better share the priceless works by its rollcall of Renaissance artists.

No urban art project evokes Florence's exciting shift in thinking quite like Manifattura Tabacchi, a stunning example of Italian Rationalist architecture designed

by Pier Luigi Nervi as a tobacco-processing plant and cigarette factory in the 1930s. Contemporary arts venues, exhibition spaces, co-working hubs, artist residencies and labs, start-ups, concept stores, a brewery, a fashion school, even a hanging rooftop garden greened with a forest of trees and a DIY recording studio kitted out to cut your own four-minute vinyl are planned for the 16 derelict hangars here. In September 2022 the curtain rises on The Factory, the central building of the Manifattura Tabacchi complex, which will serve as the collaborative hub of this forward-thinking interdisciplinary arts, fashion and counter-culture

WHEN TO GO

MAY & JUN, SEP & OCT
Late spring and autumn are warm and sunny, with festivals aplenty.

NOV-MAR
Rain, sun, occasional snow: anything goes. Some hotels and restaurants close.

APR, JUL & AUG
Easter ushers in warm days, unlike high summer when the sizzling city empties of locals and many restaurants shut.

collective. If the sassy show streamed on YouTube in 2021 to celebrate the start of construction work is anything to go by, it will be an absolutely spectacular work of art.

REBIRTH AT THE PONTE VECCHIO

The last word goes to the Medici family, the powerful dynasty of bankers and art aficionados who dominated life in 15th- to 18th-century Florence and transformed the city into the captivating Renaissance wonder that it still

is today. Following six years of uncertainty and a €10 million restoration, Florence's famous Vasari Corridor, which has connected the Uffizi gallery with Palazzo Pitti almost 1km away across the River Arno since 1565, reopens in 2022, allowing visitors to once more follow in the footsteps of the illustrious Medici along the covered passageway hidden atop the Ponte Vecchio. A sight that was once the preserve of the few will be another reason to bring the many back to the city.

Above: spanning the River Arno since 1565, Florence's restored Ponte Vecchio reopens to visitors in 2022.

Left: originally gracing the Piazza della Signoria, Michelangelo's iconic David now resides in the Galleria dell'Accademia.

Previous spread: frescoes inside the Duomo's cupola.

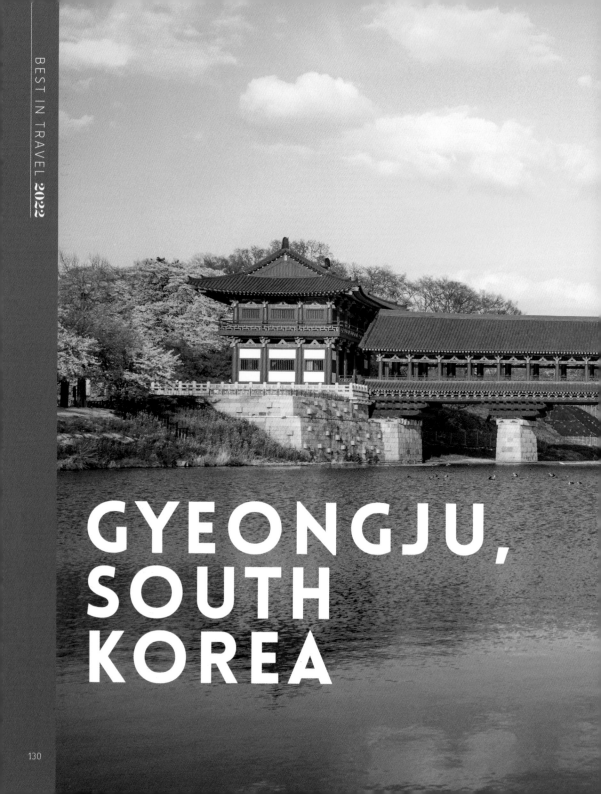

GYEONGJU, SOUTH KOREA

UTC +9hr

South Korean won

Korean

The nearest international airports are in Busan and Seoul, which both have direct airport shuttle buses to Gyeongju, along with the new rail connections.

• *Kyongju: City of Millennial History* Korean National Commission for Unesco
• *The Shaman Sorceress* Kim Dong-ni
• *Gyeongju: The Capital of Golden Silla* Sarah Milledge Nelson

Going on a treasure hunt of ancient royal artefacts in Gyeongju is a wonderful way to re-engage with travel after the pandemic lockdowns. The open-air palaces and grassy tombs of the Silla nobility, plus hundreds of Buddhist relics adorning a wild swathe of national parks, hills and lotus ponds make this 'museum without walls' a must-see and a peaceful contrast to Korea's crowded cities. Plus new train links make it all simpler than ever to visit.

DISCOVERING ROYALTY IN NATURE

Gazing across the historical centre of the coastal city of Gyeongju for the first time is like entering a Korean fairy story. This is where the Silla dynasty ruled eastern and southern Korea for the whole of the first millennium CE, their legacy visible in the many historic remains.

From 57 BCE to 935 CE, Gyeongju was the prosperous, cultural jewel of the Silla kingdom. It was the last stop on the maritime Silk Road, a place connected with far-distant empires and one to which traders brought incense and gems, Persian textiles and gold. Today, surrounding grassy tumuli tombs, there are traces of this rich past: a statue of what could only be an Arab merchant; glass bowls from ancient Rome; and Silla jewellery incorporating metalwork techniques imported from Egypt.

HIKE BACK IN TIME

Gyeongju is truly a place to slow your pace, breathe in and revel in nature, a world away from South Korea's hectic capital Seoul and busy second city Busan. In the capital, the National Museum of Korea presents objects in glass cases; in Gyeongju similar pieces can be appreciated in context, in rock carvings, pagodas and Buddhist-relic-dotted trails that cover a huge 1323 sq km. Highrise buildings are banned, meaning the low-level city centre works on a more human scale too and feels like an immersive outdoor theme park based on its regal Silla past.

This is the historic heart of Gyeongju, where Silla rulers once lived at the Wolseong Palace compound, a vast patchwork of royal pleasure gardens, fortress ruins, Asia's oldest astronomical observatory and forests. Pyramid-like green tumuli burial mounds roll across the landscape and immediately draw the eye. Preserved within are the tombs of Silla kings and queens and their treasures (as well as their servants) – setting foot inside and feeling the

Royal tombs in Tumuli-gongwon.

HIGHLIGHTS

1 **Tumuli-gongwon** Huge park whose 23 hillock-like tombs echo the mountains outside town.

2 **Bulguk-sa** The crowning glory of Silla architecture, this terraced temple sits amid trees and gardens.

3 **Seokguram** Unesco-listed grotto above Bulguk-sa where a Buddha sculpture protects the country.

4 **Namsan** Hike this lovely mountain, strewn with temple sites and Buddhas.

5 **Wolji Pond** Former royal pleasure garden, its palace spectacularly lit up at night.

Map labels:

Gyeongju National Park (Sogeumgang District)

LAKE BOMUN RESORT

Lake Bomun

Gyeongju National Park (Toham-san District)

Tumuli-gongwon **1**

5 **Wolji Pond**

Lake Bomun

Gyeongju National Park (Seoak District)

YANGBUK-MYEON

Gyeongju National Park (Toham-san District)

▲ Toham-san (745m)

Namsan (466m)

Seokguram **3**

4 ▲

Namsan

Gyeongju National Park (Namsan District)

2 **Bulguk-sa**

BULGUK-DONG

Bulguksa

Pleasure gardens of the Silla dynasty, Gyeongju's Wolji Pond is serene by day and spectacularly lit up at night.

temperature cool is part of an extraordinary sensory experience.

Outside of town, squat mountains hide Buddhist relics lost in waves of incense smoke and a soundtrack of birdsong. During the Silla period, Buddhism flowed from China into Korea through Gyeongju – objects connected to this time, and to the shamanism that preceded it, can be seen on the many hiking trails of Namsan in Unesco-designated Gyeongju National Park. Centuries of morning mists and sunshine have had a visible impact, cracking paint on deity murals and the patina on Buddha reliefs. You could spend days uncovering this splendid union of history, art, spirituality and nature.

Equally fantastical is Bulguk-sa temple, the masterpiece of Silla architecture and yet another World Heritage Site, built by a Silla monarch to appease the spirits of his parents. Walking the arched stone bridge where willow trees dip into lotus ponds is like stepping back in time.

CONNECTING WITH THE PAST AND THE FUTURE

Though a popular escape from the country's busier cities for Korean tourists, Gyeongju sees few foreign travellers. For now. In 2021, Singyeongju Station, 3km south of central Gyeongju, was connected directly to the subway networks of Busan and Pohang. Visitors can now zip from Busan to Gyeongju in just an hour, and there are talks of a shuttle tram from Singyeongju to the historic centre. At the same time, new energy-efficient high-speed trains whisk visitors here in only two hours from Seoul.

Transport developments run side by side with cultural conservation and long-term eco-friendly planning. A local government initiative supports young food-stall owners in the city to revive Korean dishes. Near the national park, sustainable-farming tourism is taking shape, encouraging visitors to stay and help grow organic produce on weekends away; these agritourism farms then donate their vegetables to local schools and communities. And along the coast, a neglected seafood warehouse is being transformed into a community centre for *haenyo* grandmother divers. The project is part of a scheme to protect this fascinating, fading profession from Jeju Island in Korea's south.

Both in its illustrious, preserved past and its plans for a future that welcomes more visitors, Gyeongju is showing that it's more than a museum without walls, a place where Korea's dazzling natural world can easily enchant the world.

WHEN TO GO

JUL-SEP
Be prepared for sweltering heat during the rainy season.

APR-JUN, OCT
Lovely temperatures and low humidity make this a great time to travel.

NOV-MAR
Snow falls and temperatures plummet making the city frigid but photogenic.

"Tumuli Park is very unique. Every day they excavate, brushing piece by piece to find treasures. Good news often comes – gold jewellery with a thousand-year history."

CLINT KWON
OWNER, HANJIN HOSTEL.

TOP
10
REGIONS

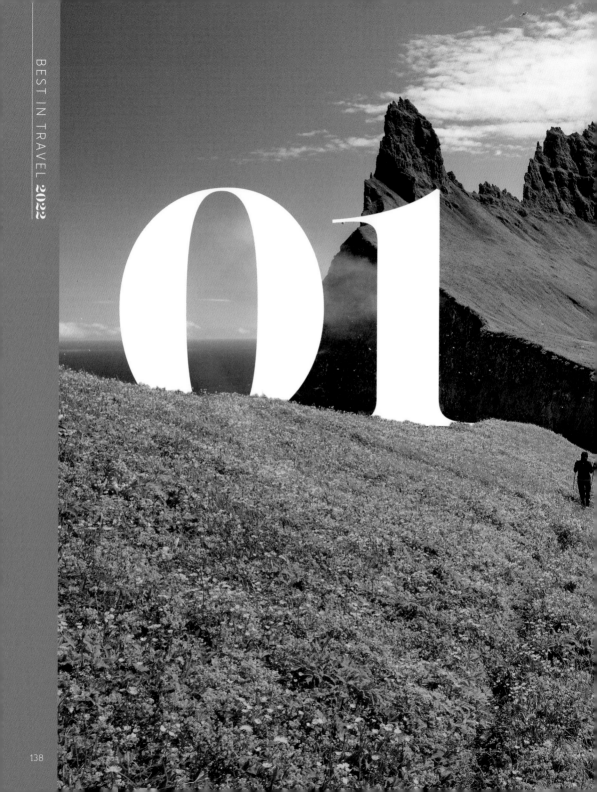

01

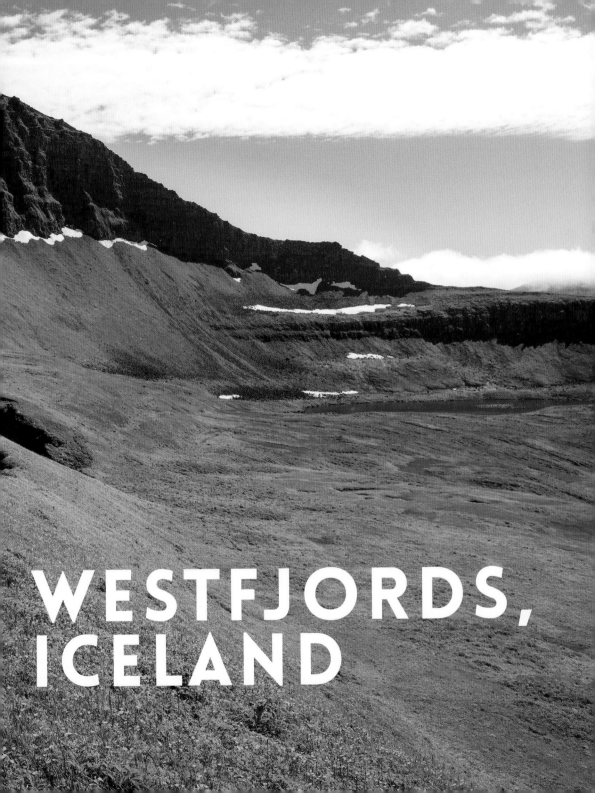

WESTFJORDS,
ICELAND

GOOD TO KNOW

UTC (no daylight savings)

Icelandic króna

Icelandic (English widely spoken)

Iceland's Keflavík International Airport has connections to Ísafjörður and Bíldudalur.

• *The Sagas of Icelanders* Various authors
• *Salka Valka* Halldór Laxness
• www.westfjords.is

In a country famous for remote, scenic spots, the Westfjords raise the bar even higher. Untouched by mass tourism and barely touched by the rest of Iceland (a 7km-wide isthmus is all that connects it to the rest of the country), the area looks like it's trying to escape, its clutch of finger-like fjords reaching out towards Greenland. Follow coast-hugging roads to explore quaint villages, spectacular landscapes, epic Icelandic history and an abundance of wildlife.

LOCAL LIFE

The small Westfjords communities founded by Viking settlers a thousand years ago have grown into, well, still small communities. As essential now as then is the need to be resourceful and self-reliant, but one big change these days is that instead of neighbour fighting neighbour in bloody feuds like those recounted in *The Sagas of Icelanders*, epic tales of the early inhabitants, communities today work together to promote and protect their precious land.

Ísafjörður, the Westfjords 'metropolis' (population 2600), is the place to begin a trip, home to museums on local life and the atmospheric, 18th-century Tjöruhúsið restaurant, where the set dinner served at communal tables feels as close to a Viking-era eating experience as you're likely to get. Businesses here and across the Westfjords are largely locally owned, know the place like the back of their hand and provide a personal service that more touristy destinations can't.

As well as keeping it local, the municipalities across the region are also thinking globally when it comes to sustainability and welcoming visitors. For over a decade they've worked with international tourism advisory group EarthCheck to meet rigorous standards, introducing initiatives including Plastic Free Westfjords and putting nature at the core of future development – efforts which have seen the region awarded Silver Certification.

NATURAL WONDERS

As the oldest part of Iceland at around 16 million years, the Westfjords have had plenty of time to perfect their natural wonders – and it's instantly obvious why the locals want to protect what they've got. The fjords that form the region's 'fingers' provide a procession of one breathtaking, stop-the-car view after another. Valleys and mountains and waterfalls are no less impressive, the latter reaching a climax at Dynjandi

HIGHLIGHTS

① **Hornstrandir Nature Reserve** Wilderness plus Arctic animals plus spirit-enhancing hiking.

② **Dynjandi** The West-fjords' most majestic, multi-tiered waterfall.

③ **Ísafjörður** Regional 'capital' with museums, restaurants and activities.

④ **Vigur** Birds, seals and cinnamon buns on a fjord-set island.

⑤ **Þingeyri Peninsula** Setting for *Gisli's Epic*, one of the most famous and bloodiest of *The Sagas of Icelanders*.

"The municipalities in the Westfjords are certified sustainable destinations. That tells me that the people here appreciate nature and want to protect the lifestyle we live. "

LÍNA TRYGGVADÓTTIR
PROJECT MANAGER, WESTFJORDS REGIONAL DEVELOPMENT OFFICE

where a wide curtain of water drops 100m down to join with smaller falls in a dazzling display. You won't want to sunbathe on Rauðisandur beach but you will want your camera ready to snap its surreal pink- and red-hued sands. Headline act is Hornstrandir Nature Reserve, the ultimate in wilderness escapes, with no transport access other than ferries from Ísafjörður, and no way of getting around other than on foot. The reward for such intrepidness is some of the most beautiful, unspoilt land- and seascapes on earth, from saw cliffs and waterfalls to wildflowers and wildlife.

And after a day's adventures, nature in the Westfjords even provides an alternative to a hotel bath with immersion in one of many geothermally heated pools – Reykjafjarðarlaug is in an especially pretty location and combines a fjord-facing pool with a delightfully warm hot-pot.

WESTFJORDS WILDLIFE
The scarcity of humans in the Westfjords has allowed species of birds and animals to thrive – or to at least have the chance to make a comeback. A latter case in point is

the endangered white-tailed eagle whose primary breeding ground is along the south coast. For more avian ogling, ornithologists flock to the Westfjords' westernmost tip, the Látrabjarg Peninsula. A 12km stretch of cliffs here sees puffins, razorbills, cormorants, guillemots and many more species nest in dizzying numbers.

More teeming birdlife and the chance to see Iceland's only

WHEN TO GO

JUN-AUG
Almost endless daylight and warm temperatures allow exploring late into the evening.

MAY & SEP
Even fewer tourists than usual and relatively reliable weather make for a good time to visit.

OCT-APR
Dark and cold, with many attractions closed, but perfect for complete solitude and spotting the Northern Lights.

native land mammal in the wild, the Arctic fox, can be found in Hornstrandir. A far easier way to see one is at the specialist centre in Súdavík, a short drive from Ísafjörður, which usually has an orphaned fox or two being cared for, along with extensive displays on them and a great café. Marine mammals relish the food-rich waters lapping the fjords. Take a boat trip from Ísafjörður and you might spot whales and dolphins out in the deep and seals on the tiny island of Vigur, also noteworthy for

its puffin population, Iceland's oldest lighthouse, sweeping Hestfjörður views – and the best cinnamon buns in the world.

Some wildlife you're unlikely to spot are the legendary sea monsters associated with the waters of Arnarfjörður – but you can visit the Bíldadalur museum's dedicated section on the Icelandic Nessie. And plan a return trip to the Westfjords for a second chance to spy one and enjoy again everything else this region has to offer.

Above: Dynjandi, the most dramatic waterfall in the Westfjords.

Left: head to the Látrabjarg Peninsula to spot huge colonies of puffins and other seabirds.

Previous spread: the island of Vigur.

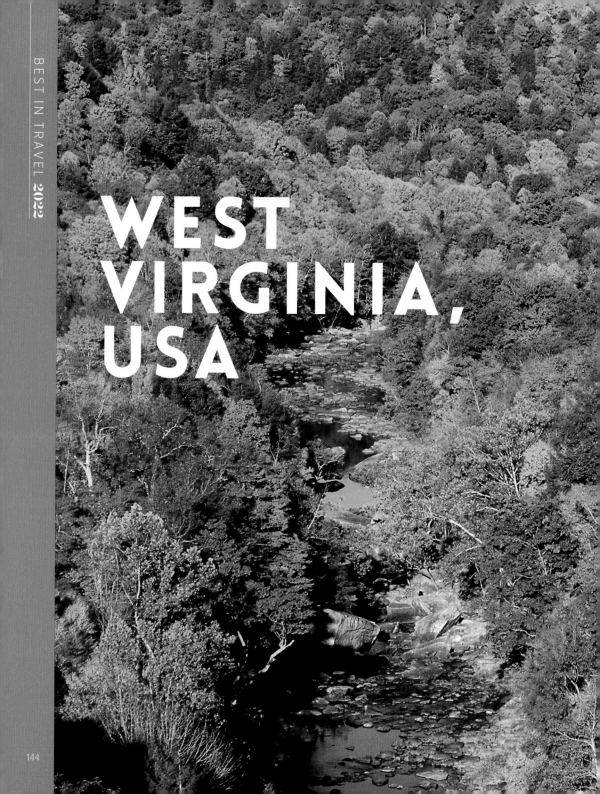

WEST VIRGINIA, USA

UTC -5hr

US dollar

English

Fly into Yeager for the capital Charleston, or Greenbrier Valley for many of the state's resorts. It's less than a five-hour drive from major cities across the East, South and Mid-Atlantic.

• *State by State: A Panoramic Portrait of America/West Virginia* Jayne Anne Phillips
• *Charleston Gazette-Mail* www.wvgazette-mail.com
• www.wvtourism.com

Split from its coastal sister during the Civil War, West Virginia has sometimes seemed overshadowed by its neighbours. But the Mountain State has long been a nexus of American culture and is finally attracting some well deserved outside attention. Visitors will discover a still-uncrowded region with unspoiled mountains and unmistakable heritage, where the leisurely tempo of Southern small towns converges with the adrenaline sports that attract adventurers from across the continent.

AN INDEPENDENT SPIRIT

Despite being connected to the rest of the US by a series of major roads, railways and airports, West Virginia has often felt isolated. Part of this is down to physical separation from bordering states by the forested ridge of the Appalachian Mountains and the serpentine Ohio River, but this is also a region that, while sitting at a cultural and geographical crossroads, has maintained a distinct Appalachian culture and heritage entirely its own.

SUSTAINABLE TOURISM EMERGES

West Virginia is shifting away from the fossil fuel production that was once the backbone of its economy and reimagining how to use the state's natural resources. Instead of being used for logging, coal and salt, its forests, mountains and caverns are now seen as the route to sustainable prosperity.

All across WV's foothills and valleys, tenacious communities have begun turning towards tourism. Visitors can explore a vast network of

caves. Abandoned railways have been revived as rail-trails and scenic train rides, such as the Cass Scenic Railroad State Park. And at Dawson Lake, an eco-resort with an agritourism hub is planned, complete with angular treehouses hewn from local timber.

This shift towards nature isn't entirely new – the state's pristine forests, parklands and preserves have long been a lure for outdoor enthusiasts. Paddlers congregate at the Gauley River for Class V rapids, particularly in September and October; or seek more leisurely boating on the Bluestone. Come winter, Snowshoe Resort has 270 acres of skiable terrain in the Allegheny Mountains.

NEW BEGINNINGS IN WEST VIRGINIA

One specific location is spearheading the region's drive towards sustainable development – the New River Gorge. Already one of West Virginia's best-known sites, the New, as it's affectionately known, was

The West Virginia State Capitol on the Kanawha River in Charleston.

HIGHLIGHTS

1 **Harpers Ferry National Historical Park** A stuck-in-time 19th-century town and a network of hiking trails.

2 **New River Gorge National Park and Preserve** Whitewater rafting, climbing and a gorge-spanning bridge.

3 **The Greenbrier** Famed resort with an on-site, Cold War-era bunker.

4 **Snowshoe Mountain** Ski or snowboard in winter, hike or bike in summer.

5 **Lost World Caverns** Easy-access or advanced-level cave network tours.

Each October, BASE jumpers congregate to leap from the steel-arched span of New River Gorge National Park's bridge.

recently reborn as the nation's newest national park, with help from a coronavirus-era stimulus package. It's a triumph for conservationists and tourism advocates who expect the upgraded status (from national river) will translate to more visitors, more revenue and more support for the park's continued preservation.

Included among the New's attractions are hiking and mountain-biking trails, miles of whitewater for kayaking, and towering sandstone cliffs with over 1500 rock climbing routes. On Bridge Day, held on the third Saturday of every October to celebrate the 1977 completion of the New River Gorge Bridge, BASE jumpers are allowed to plunge 267m from the iconic steel arch that stretches across the gorge.

A HISTORY TO REMEMBER
Even while looking forward, there are opportunities to learn about West Virginia's past. At the New and across southern WV, visitors can drive the self-guided African American Heritage Tour to learn the stories of the Black miners, railroad workers and others who were instrumental in the development of Appalachia, and hear about the music created in the coal camps stamped across the mountains here.

Over in the northeast of the state is Harpers Ferry, a historical park where the Potomac and Shenandoah rivers converge (you can see clear across into Maryland and Virginia) and where abolitionist John Brown attempted to incite a revolt against slavery in 1859.

And the Adena Mound at the Grave Creek Mound Archaeological Complex in the north is an impressive, 2000-year-old reminder that people lived and relied on this land long before Europeans arrived.

A HISTORY TO REMEMBER
West Virginia doesn't have any big cities – even its capital, Charleston, has shrunk to under 50,000 people – and the entire state's population has been in a decade-long decline. But a new programme that invites remote workers to move here could signal a turning tide – and give communities the tools to encourage others to stay.

Considered a strategy for long-term talent acquisition, Ascend West Virginia is offering $12,000 and a series of other perks to people who relocate to Morgantown, a college town home to West Virginia University, for at least two consecutive years. Future applicants will be considered for idyllic Shepherdstown and Lewisburg, an artsy enclave in the state's southeast.

To many, West Virginia is defined by these small towns, where fiercely proud families have lived for generations. But the state's future may rely on it welcoming out-of-towners not just for a single visit to enjoy its many attractions, but long enough to call the Mountain State home.

WHEN TO GO

JUN-OCT
High season, though summer can get hot and humid. For milder temperatures and fall foliage, visit in autumn.

NOV-FEB
Expect snowfall and fog when temperatures drop, but this is a great time to hit the slopes.

MAR-MAY
Mild temperatures and rain are common during the spring season, along with wildflower blooms.

"The national park brand allows us to share New River Gorge with a broader audience in hopes that when they see and fall in love with the place, they'll help us protect it."

EVE WEST, NEW RIVER GORGE NATIONAL PARK AND PRESERVE

XISHUANGBA CHINA

NNA,

03

GOOD TO KNOW

UTC +8hr

Chinese Yuan Renminbi

Mandarin Chinese, Dai, Bulang, Buxing, Kemie, Hu

Jinghong is the central transit point for Xishuangbanna. Flights, buses and the new trains connect the city to Yunnan, surrounding Chinese provinces, and Laos, Thailand and Vietnam.

• *South of the Clouds: Tales from Yunnan* Lucien Miller (ed)
• *Simply Yunnan: Simple Ingredients, Simple Technique* Rebecca Henderson
• *Across Yunnan: A Journey of Surprises* Archibald John Little

The wide, slow current of the Lancang (Mekong) River has long epitomised the quiet pace of life in the market towns and remote tropical jungles of Southwest China's Xishuangbanna prefecture – but that appears to be changing. Intensive domestic investment in tourism infrastructure and the completion of the high-speed China-Laos Railway project have put Xishuangbanna on track to regain its ancient status as a central hub of Southeast Asian travel and trade.

ON, OFF AND BACK ON THE BEATEN TRACK

A remote corner of Southwest China's Yunnan province, culturally closer to Bangkok than Beijing, Xishuangbanna has spent the past decade undergoing a transformation from offbeat backpacker destination to hub of domestic tourism. Once an important stop on the ancient Tea Horse Road, a transport route built on the trade of tea leaves and thoroughbreds between Tibet and Southeast Asia, massive modern tourism infrastructure investments are bringing 'Banna once more to the fore.

The region has become a hot commodity among Chinese tourists, lured by year-round warm weather, diverse minority cultural traditions and equally diverse and delicious cuisines related to Southeast Asian peoples rather than Han Chinese, and an explosion of international hotel groups building flashy new resorts. All of it without needing to cross an international border – and soon without even needing to board a plane.

Once little more than a footnote in travel guides to Yunnan Province, and seen as much as a backdoor route to Laos and Vietnam as a destination in its own right, Xishuangbanna slowly gained a reputation among international travellers for jungle treks to remote villages deep in the hills. In modern times, rubber and banana plantations have pushed the jungle further and further back, while the government has made huge efforts to connect even the remotest villages by road – though these trips can admittedly still be harrowing on a swaying local bus on narrow mountain roads. Few these days come for trekking, however; far more visit for the culture.

DELICIOUS DIVERSITY

Xishuangbanna is home to fourteen of China's fifty-five official ethnic minorities – the Dai group being most numerous at around a quarter

HIGHLIGHTS

1 Dai Water Splashing Festival, Jinghong Mid-April new year celebrations that get wet and wild.

2 Xiding Market The best of Xishuangbanna's weekly village markets, way off the tourist track.

3 Tropical Plant Gardens, Menglun China's largest botanical gardens mixes the manicured with the wild.

4 Damenglong Explore Dai culture and religion at these twin temples.

5 Xinghuoshan Snap 'Banna's photogenic Pu'er tea plantations.

> **"Xishuangbanna is a destination of tropical rainforests, wild elephants, a culture closely related to that of the Thai and some of the best cuisine that China has to offer."**
>
> YERETH JANSEN
> CEO, GOKUNMING.COM

of the population. And each of the fourteen is sub-divided into further self-identifying groups not explicitly included in China's *minzu* classifications. All of which makes this region a beautiful blend of cultures and customs. Though domestic travellers largely stick to theme-park-like model villages – where it's possible to see the famous annual Dai Water Splashing Festival daily at 3pm – visitors in search of a more authentic experience can still head to the hills on local transport. Though separated by only a few dozen kilometres of winding mountain roads, differences between the ethnic groups can be pronounced and outsiders will most easily distinguish the various cultural communities by their female fashions: Dai women typically wear bright skirts and sarongs wrapped by silver belts; Jinuo tend towards striped tunics and black skirts accented with plenty of jewellery; Bulang and Hani are most easily recognised by elaborate headdresses – for the former these are decorated with fresh flowers, for the latter with coins and rings.

Common across all these cultures is excellent food that combine Chinese and Southeast Asian influences and ingredients to make it among the tastiest in the region. Barbecued fish, lemongrass sauces, fried bananas served with an unhealthy but delicious dollop of sticky-sweet condensed milk, and locally harvested coffee all mean visits never lack flavour. Tea lovers too are drawn to the area – fermented Pu'er tea is still grown and processed in the eponymous region next door, which while not administratively part of Xishuangbanna offers a remarkably similar travel experience for visitors.

LETTING THE TRAIN TAKE THE STRAIN

Long limited by the lack of

WHEN TO GO

NOV-APR
Lower temperatures and little rain mean ideal conditions for jungle treks and village visits.

SEP & OCT
Quite warm and rainy; smaller crowds make this period appealing.

MAY-AUG
Expect sudden violent downpours in the hottest and rainiest months of the year.

connectivity to the rest of China, much of Xishuangbanna's boom has been thanks to the growing number of transport connections linking the region to the wider world. Overnight bus rides from Kunming have become one-hour flights, with options from Jinghong Airport now also linking the region directly to major cities across China as well as to Cambodia, Laos and Thailand. Most significant though, the China-Laos Railway, completed at the end of 2021, connects Jinghong by high-speed train to Kunming and Vientiane, capital of Laos – later stages of the project are planned to continue onwards to Thailand and eventually all the way to Singapore.

Though the Tibetan horses and Pu'er brews of the ancient Tea Horse Road may no longer be the major commodities, this increased connectivity should once again see Xishuangbanna back as a crucial interchange of people and goods between China and Southeast Asia – a cultural connection that locals never quite left behind anyway.

Above: Xishuangbanna promises a culinary tour of Southeast Asia, from barbecued fish to the more unusual offerings of traditional Dai cuisine.

Left: hibiscus at Menglun's Tropical Plant Gardens.

Previous spread: pagodas are painted with traditional Dai designs.

KENT'S HERITAGE COAST, ENGLAND

© PREVIOUS PAGE: CATUNCIA | SHUTTERSTOCK; ABOVE: IAN WOOLCOCK | SHUTTERSTOCK

GOOD TO KNOW

UTC

British pound

English

Dover and Folkestone are on the high-speed train line from London's St Pancras Station. Folkestone is also connected to France via the Channel Tunnel.

• *The Darling Buds of May* HE Bates
• www.kentdowns.org.uk/our-projects/unesco-sites-of-the-channel
• www.creativefolkestone.org.uk

Already a recognised Area of Outstanding Natural Beauty (AONB), the English county of Kent's Downs and Heritage Coast are now looking at Unesco World Heritage Site status. Long stretches of beautiful, iconic white cliffs, the regeneration of its two main towns, historic Dover and creative Folkestone, and idyllic countryside bordering it are all excellent reasons to believe it will achieve its goal – and a 2022 Landscape Festival makes it a good reason to visit now.

CROSS-CHANNEL CONFLICT

The peace and quiet of the Kent Downs and Heritage Coast today stand in stark contrast to its dramatic history. Looking out across the English Channel towards France, this region has been the frontline of defence for England over the centuries, usually successfully, sometimes not – William the Conqueror and his army rampaged through the area on the way to London after winning the 1066 Battle of Hastings nearby. Dover Castle was built by the Normans and nicknamed the 'Key to England', such was its strategic importance during centuries of cross-Channel conflict. In WWII this stretch of shoreline became a symbol of resilience and hope to the British – with Nazi-occupied France clearly visible across the water and the threat of invasion looming, the White Cliffs of Dover became an icon, with a namesake song made famous by by Dame Vera Lynn ensuring an enduring place in the British psyche ever since.

CROSS-CHANNEL COOPERATION

Fast forward eight decades and instead of the Kent coast keeping its distance from its French counterpart, it's actively embracing it. Not content with just being an Area of Outstanding Natural Beauty, the Kent Downs team are looking into Unesco World Heritage Site status, working in partnership with similar organisations across La Manche in France. With financial support from the European Union and led by the Armorique Regional Nature Park in Brittany, the Unesco Sites of the Channel project is a collaboration involving several regions in northern France and southern England to celebrate their shared heritage and natural wonders. Kent hopes to promote the region as a sustainable tourism destination to the benefit of local communities and visitors alike, with the Kent Downs AONB becoming a Global Geopark or Biosphere Reserve, and the Strait of Dover

Folkestone harbour has a newly restored promenade.

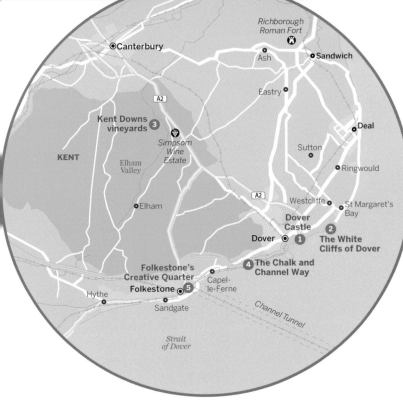

HIGHLIGHTS

❶ Dover Castle Two thousand years of history and views of the Channel.

❷ White Cliffs of Dover Iconic symbols of wartime resilience and England's 'Welcome Home' sign.

❸ Kent Downs vineyards Chalky soil produces Champagne-like fizz.

❹ The Chalk and Channel Way Cliff-top biking, hiking and art between Dover and Folkestone.

❺ Folkestone's Creative Quarter An artistic hub centred in the pretty Old Town of this seaside resort.

Explore WWII-era tunnels at Dover Castle, built during its stint as a military command centre.

becoming a World Heritage Site. To highlight the ongoing work, a 2022 Landscape Festival aims to use art and outdoor events to engage and excite participants in sustainable ways, helping them value this irreplaceable landscape, while the EXPERIENCE project is supporting local businesses in developing new off-season, low-environmental impact tourism experiences.

KENTISH DELIGHTS

So what can visitors expect? The aforementioned Dover Castle is a clear historic highlight. The present building is over 800 years old and the cliffs under it were used during WWII as a hospital and military command centre, but the site's origin's as a defensive site might go back 2000 years to an Iron Age hill fort. The Romans recognised the area's importance as the closest point to mainland Europe (just 33km away) by constructing a still-largely-intact lighthouse here. Today, the castle looks down on a regeneration scheme that will see the upgrade of Dover's marina and the renovation of the town's Market Square.

The coast's other main town, Folkestone, has less historical interest but plenty of contemporary artistic appeal. Its pretty Old Town has been dubbed the Creative Quarter, a self-proclaimed 'urban village' where 90 of the buildings lining its cobblestone streets have been turned into shops, cafes and artist studios thanks to the concerted efforts of the local community. Watch painters at work

or sign up to an art class before enjoying dinner in a chic bistro or a performance in one of the bars.

Connecting the two seaside towns, the Heritage Coast is best explored by bike or on foot following the sometimes steep, 11km-long Chalk and Channel Way, part of Route 2 on the National Cycle Network. Let the views distract you from the uphill bits – try to spot France on the horizon – and look out for artworks along the way too.

Heading inland, the Kent Downs section of the AONB offers a quintessential English landscape of rolling hills, fields and woods – along with some less quintessentially English vineyards. Elham Valley and Simpsons grow grapes on chalky soil similar to that in the Champagne region, producing quality sparkling wines with a growing reputation. Making a diversion along sun-dappled country lanes to get to them is well worth it – and you can raise a glass of bubbly to the region's Unesco bid while you're there

WHEN TO GO

JUN-AUG
Warm weather for outdoor pursuits but busy during the school holidays.

MAY & SEP
Reliably good weather and fewer tourists make this the best time to visit.

OCT-APR
Cooler and wetter weather make for atmospheric, quieter exploration.

"The enchanting Kent Downs are home to rare grassland, wild orchids, ancient woodlands, peaceful villages, historic churches and castles, and fossil seams whose chalk is exposed as world famous white cliffs."

NICK JOHANNSEN
DIRECTOR, KENT DOWNS AREA OF OUTSTANDING NATURAL BEAUTY

PUERTO RICO

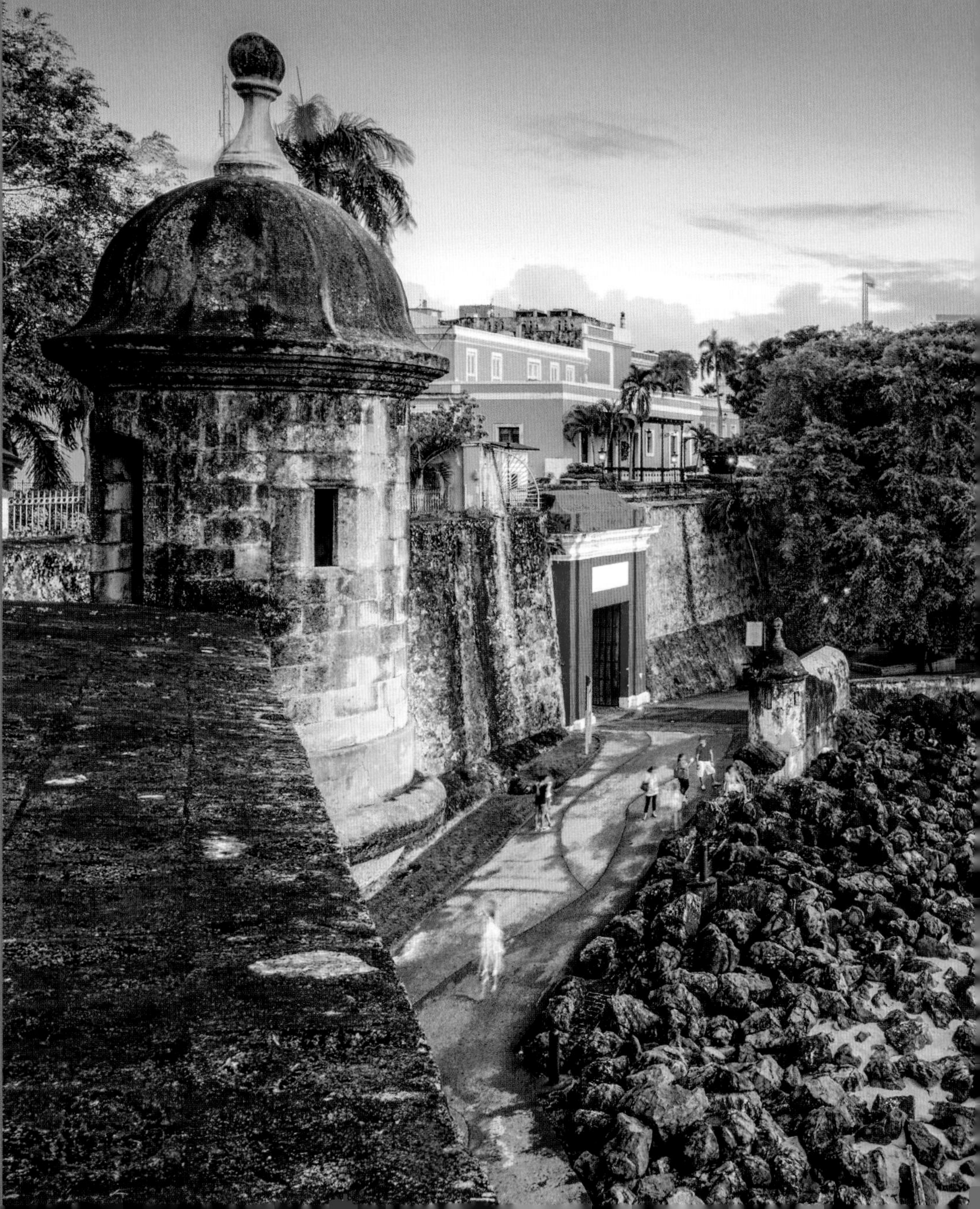

GOOD TO KNOW

UTC -4hr

US dollar

Spanish, English

Puerto Rico is the Caribbean's most accessible island. Luis Muñoz Marín International Airport has flights from most major American hubs. San Juan is the western hemisphere's second-largest cruise ship port after Miami.

• *When I was Puerto Rican* Esmeralda Santiago
• *We Fed an Island: The True Story of Rebuilding Puerto Rico, One Meal at a Time* José Andrés
• *Simone* Eduardo Lalo

Puerto Rico is an ideal place to warm your soul and revive your spirits. Year-round sun, uplifting tropical rhythms and sloth-inducing beaches are the standard crowd-pleasers. And under that appealing surface more elusive and nuanced draws are there to discover: a steely toughness, a rock-solid sense of community and the notion that, after hurricanes and earthquakes, this remarkable little archipelago knows how to weather a storm and pull through.

THE RESILIENT ISLAND

The last few years have not been kind to Puerto Rico, an unincorporated territory of the USA. Hit by a once-in-a-century storm, a sequence of damaging seismic events and the global coronavirus pandemic, the challenges have rained down thick and fast. But thanks to the spirit of its people, who have responded with optimism and ingenuity to successive crises, a slow but steady recovery is underway. The so-called Charming Island (Isla del Encanto) is also the resilient island.

Puerto Rico's rebuilding after 2017's Hurricane Maria and the 2019 earthquakes hasn't just brought people together, it's also made the territory more inventive and self-sufficient. Behind the harrowing news stories lie encouraging tales of tenacity and creativity. There's the Vieques craft-distillery that makes coffee-flavoured rum in an old US Navy fire station; the gourmet farm-to-table restaurants that are embracing local crop-growers to ensure future food security; and the dazzling murals of San Juan's Santurce neighbourhood that have transformed a neglected warehouse district into an outdoor art gallery.

While recent events might have brought pain and heartache, they've also prompted healing. Changed but not broken by successive disasters, the Boricuas (Puerto Ricans) have adapted to their different circumstances and emerged more determined than ever to live life to the full.

BEYOND THE RESORTS

This US territory has long been popular for its manicured golf courses and glitzy casinos. But savvy travellers with time to spare have discovered the advantages of eschewing the shiny macro resorts for smaller micro businesses. Much of the joy of Puerto Rico lies in its local haunts. Beyond the tourist enclaves, the territory's three-pronged Spanish, African and Native Taino heritage

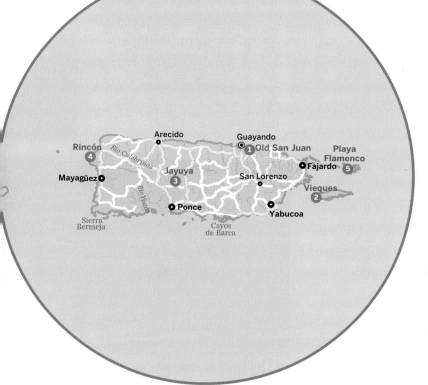

HIGHLIGHTS

1 **Old San Juan** Spanish colonial streets, plazas, forts and mansions overlaid with a vibrant modern buzz.

2 **Vieques** Seek out beaches, cool sleeping options and a sparkling bioluminescent bay.

3 **Jayuya** Coffee farms, archaeological sites and a rum distillery enliven this de facto mountain capital.

4 **Rincón** Ride the Tres Palmas breaks at the Caribbean's top surf town.

5 **Playa Flamenco** Calm, clear waters at a sublime Culebra island beach.

> "Our island's amazing and unique cultural heritage, astounding natural beauty and diversity, combined with its modern infrastructure, make it an ideal destination for your must-visit list."

CARLOS MERCADO SANTIAGO
EXECUTIVE DIRECTOR, PUERTO RICO TOURISM COMPANY.

manifests itself in diminutive towns and crinkled countryside. The mountains guard small-scale coffee farms and pre-Columbian archaeological sites. The coast offers evocatively named surf spots and splendidly restored lighthouses.

If there's a mantra for a traveller heading here in 2022 it should be 'stay longer, dig deeper'. After exploring the El Yunque rainforest, still recovering after Hurricane Maria, take in the unusual tropical dry forest of Guánica on the south coast. When you're done visiting Old San Juan's colossal forts, stroll the architecturally lavish streets of historic San Germán in the southwest.

TIMELESS MELODIES

Culturally, Puerto Rico exhibits the diversity and sophistication of a much larger country, especially in the realm of music. Rapper Daddy Yankee is credited with inventing the term 'reggaeton' in the 1990s. Dragged into the mainstream, the once subversive music of San Juan's housing projects and *marquesinas* (carports) has come a long way since its underground beginnings. These days you won't get far in Puerto Rico without hearing the strains of local boy turned international star, Bad Bunny, the most streamed music artist in the world in 2020.

The diaspora has produced its own melody makers: J-Lo is so famous her name only needs three letters; Marc Anthony redefined tropical salsa in the 1990s and 2000s; and Lin-Manuel Miranda, creator of the musical *Hamilton,* is arguably the greatest songsmith of the last decade in any genre.

BACK ON THE MENU

Puerto Rico's food culture has been simmering for over a decade. If you've never heard of *mofongo,* it's time you sampled the rich plantain-based mash-up once hailed by chef Anthony Bourdain as a 'tower of

WHEN TO GO

DEC-APR
Cooler and drier
than summer; March
has the least rain and
lowest humidity.

JUN-SEP
Hot, humid and wet.
Historically, Sep-
tember is the worst
month for hurricanes.

MAY, OCT & NOV
Temperatures and
rainfall pick up in
May, but storm threat
remains low; October
carries a risk of
hurricanes.

goodness'. In the prestigious 2019 James Beard Awards, three Puerto Rican chefs were nominated for honours, among them Jose Enrique, a homegrown culinary maestro who recently moved his acclaimed San Juan restaurant from Santurce to Condado. A passionate promoter of the farm-to-fork ethos using *ingredients del país* (from the country), Enrique's star rose to new heights when, in the wake of Hurricane Maria, he was one of several restaurateurs who teamed up with Spanish-American chef José Andrés to provide thousands of Puerto Ricans with free meals – locally sourced sandwiches, paella and stew were dispatched from food trucks and mobile kitchens around the country.

Such actions were the start of a rebound in fortunes and a reignition of the territory's traditional enthusiasm and verve. Puerto Rico is back on the menu in 2022 – stronger, more versatile but still with all the *encanto* that has charmed visitors over the years.

Above: one of Puerto Rico's crown jewels, El Yunque boasts nearly 29,000 acres of lush mountainous terrain.

Left: Los Morrillos Lighthouse, overlooking the Refugio Nacional Cabo Rojo on Puerto Rico's southwest coast.

Previous spread: surfing at Condado Beach.

06

SHIKOKU,
JAPAN

Japan's fourth largest island provides an intriguing opportunity to get off the main tourist trails and get behind the *tatemae*, the public face of Japan, and discover examples of the country's *honne*, the private face that few foreigners are privileged to glimpse unless they take a few detours. On Shikoku, a real sense of community can be explored on an ancient Buddhist pilgrimage, in Japan's first 'zero-waste' town and in the remote, 'hidden' Iya Valley.

GOOD TO KNOW

UTC +9hr

Yen

Japanese

Three bridges link Shikoku to the main island of Honshū, with train and bus connections. Visitors can get to the island by ferry too, and each of Shikoku's four major cities (Matsuyama, Kōchi, Takamatsu and Tokushima) has an airport.

• *Japanese Pilgrimage* Oliver Statler
• *Botchan* Natsume Sōseki
• *Lost Japan* Alex Kerr

88 SACRED TEMPLES OF SHIKOKU PILGRIMAGE

Henro, or pilgrims, have been walking around Shikoku for 1200 years in their search for enlightenment, following in the footsteps of the Shingon Buddhist saint Kōbō Daishi, who achieved nirvana here. While these days most *henro* complete the 1400km pilgrimage in a car or bus, there are still plenty willing to undertake the quest on foot.

A prime example of the feeling of 'community' on Shikoku is that, despite hosting walking *henro* for over a millennium, the custom of *settai* – contributing to a pilgrim's efforts on their quest for enlightenment – is alive and well.

It may involve an old woman crossing the road to press 10 yen into the hand of a walking pilgrim. Or a driver stopping and passing a can of cold soda to a *henro* on a hot day. Or it might be a priest not charging walking pilgrims to stamp and sign their temple book. The giver says 'o-settai shimasu' and the pilgrim cannot refuse this contribution from the heart, an effort by the giver to feel a part of the pilgrim's endeavour.

The people of Shikoku are proud of their island's pilgrimage. It has a long and endearing history. And those setting off on the challenge should remember the words of Kōbō Daishi: 'Do not just walk in the footsteps of the men of old, seek what they sought.'

THE 'ZERO-WASTE' TOWN

The small town of Kamikatsu, tucked away in the forested mountains of eastern Shikoku, is making its own efforts to achieve enlightenment by being Japan's first 'zero-waste' town. Residents compost all of their organic waste matter, while rubbish is sorted into a mind-boggling 45 categories at the town's Gomi (Trash) Station.

In 2019, 80% of the town's waste was recycled, compared to Japan's national average of 20%. There's

Follow the coast road around Shikoku.

HIGHLIGHTS

1 **Iya Valley** Cross swaying vine bridges in gorgeous isolation in the depths of this secluded valley.

2 **Ishizuchi-san** Climb a sacred mountain via steel chains and steps.

3 **Dōgo Onsen** An historic onsen (hot spring) in the castle-town of Matsuyama.

4 **Naoshima** Marvel at the meeting of nature and contemporary art on this island in the Inland Sea.

5 **Ōkinohama** A beach that's good for surfing, bobbing in the waves or just relaxing.

Immerse in Kami-katsu living via the INOW programme, pitching in with the locals and enjoying fabulous food at homestays.

an attitude that 'zero-waste' and sustainability are part of becoming enlightened and feeling happy with yourself, your community and your town. Just as the *henro* makes an effort on their pilgrimage, the individual makes an effort in their community for the benefit of all. Making that effort may require spending time, energy and money, but the payback in terms of quality of life make it more than worthwhile.

Kamikatsu has taken this a step further, with the INOW programme. Meaning 'let's go home' (and pronounced 'ee-no' in the local dialect), it gives visitors the chance to become locals for two weeks. Participants contribute to the town, living a zero-waste lifestyle, taking part in activities such as sorting garbage at the Gomi Station, helping with seasonal jobs such as harvesting tea and spending time with inspiring, talented locals. It's all about bettering yourself and contributing to the community. If this concept in travel appeals, see www.inowkamikatsu.com.

THE 'HIDDEN' IYA VALLEY

The central Shikoku mountains boast steep gorges, twisting rivers and cliff-hanging roads. The Iya Valley here is known as the last refuge of members of the vanquished Heike clan following defeat in the late 12th century. Legend says the escaping warriors disappeared into the valley, building wisteria vine bridges (*kazura-bashi*) that could be swiftly chopped down if need be to stop enemies pursuing them.

The twin *kazura-bashi* at East-Iya are a joy to behold, inaccessible to tour buses thanks to narrow, winding Rte 439 that keeps the two bridges off most itineraries. Visitors will need their own wheels to get here, but this remote part of the Iya Valley rewards the effort.

The tiny village of Nagoro is another eye-opener. Those 'people' waiting at the bus stop, chatting on a porch and working in the fields are actually *kakashi*, incredibly life-like scarecrow-type dolls, made by villagers to commemorate former friends and relatives, and to combat loneliness brought about by the depopulation of the village. Rural exodus is a major problem in Japan, with young people heading off to the cities, and as older people pass on, rural villages like Nagoro die with them. Nagoro's response was to repopulate with life-size dolls – giving the visitor another example of that *honne*, or private face of Japan, that most miss out on if they don't get off the well-beaten track and away from the big cities.

© JUNICHI MIYAZAKI | LONELY PLANET

WHEN TO GO

APR & MAY, AUG-NOV
Spring is for pilgrimages; August for festivals; autumn for fall colours.

JUN & JUL
Nobody likes the sticky rainy season, especially walking pilgrims.

DEC-MAR
Wintery and cold, especially on the Pacific coast.

"Shikoku has beautiful scenery, rich history and culture and ancient Buddhist pilgrimage trails. It's an enchanting blend of old and new Japan."

MITSUYO MORIKAWA
SHIKOKU TRAVEL CONCIERGE

07

ATACAMA DESERT, CHILE

GOOD TO KNOW

UTC -6hr

Chilean peso

Spanish, plus many
indigenous languages

From capital Santiago
regional flights head
to Calama, the near-
est airport to the
Atacama, and a hub
for buses and tour
operators. Alterna-
tively, catch a long-
haul bus or rent a car
in Santiago

• www.chile.travel
• www.astroturismo
chile.travel
• www.cielo-thefilm.
com

If there's one thing everyone's searching for in the Covid era, it's space. And for emptiness, it's hard to top the Atacama Desert, South America's oldest, highest and driest desert. With its lunar-like landscapes, strange life-forms and extra-terrestrial colours, it's the closest most people will ever get to stepping onto another planet. Appropriately enough, it's also one of the world's premier spots for stargazing – as well as one of Chile's leading lights for sustainable tourism.

A WINDOW ON THE STARS

Stretching north to south for 1600km, and west from Chile's Pacific coastline east to the foothills of the Andes, the vast and empty Atacama puts the desert in deserted. As one of the least populated areas in the country, it's an ideal place for socially distanced adventures, but there's another compelling reason to visit – the clarity of the night skies.

Sandwiched between the cool currents of the Pacific and the high, rain-blocking peaks of the Andes, the Atacama's skies are astonishingly free of clouds (parts of the desert receive less than 1mm of rainfall a year). Factor in the lack of light pollution and the high altitude – in excess of 4000m in some areas – and you have one of the best locations on Earth for stargazing.

Unsurprisingly then, the region is home to some of the world's most important observatories, including the Atacama Large Millimeter Array (ALMA), the largest radio telescope ever built, consisting of 66 giant parabolic dishes that enable astronomers to peer into some of the deepest, darkest corners of our galaxy. The desert's newest observatory, the Fred Young Submillimeter Telescope (named after an alumnus of Cornell University), was completed in 2021.

Thankfully, you don't have to be a professional to appreciate the show. Tour companies like Una Noche con las Estrellas offer nightly star safaris, and several observatories are open to visitors, including the Paranal Observatory, with free public tours every Saturday; and ALMA itself, with a fascinating visitor centre open at weekends where you can chat to staff and observe the laboratories and control room.

Another superb starspotting location is the Elqui Valley, near the Atacama's southern edge. The small town of Vicuña makes the ideal base, with the Observatorio Cerro

HIGHLIGHTS

1 **San Pedro de Atacama** Surf sand dunes, snap sapphire lakes and see sunsets at this lively desert town.

2 **El Tatio geysers** Visit the world's highest-altitude geyser field.

3 **Elqui Valley** Explore observatories, quiet villages and *pisco* distilleries.

4 **Reserva Nacional Los Flamencos** Salt flats, lunar ridges, topaz lakes and mountain peaks.

5 **Parque Nacional Nevado Tres Cruces** Hike amid high-Andean lagoons and herds of *guanacos*.

> **Thanks to the Atacama's elevation, lack of light pollution and clear skies, you can usually see around 4500 stars with the naked eye. Often you can even distinguish individual colours.**

DANIEL RODRIGUEZ
PROFESSIONAL STAR GUIDE, UNA NOCHE CON LAS ESTRELLAS

Mamalluca and Observatorio del Pangue both nearby. Personalised stargazing is also offered by the enthusiastic astronomers at Alfa Aldea.

2022 has a couple of astronomical events to look out for: a partial solar eclipse in April and a total lunar eclipse in May. Cross those fingers for clear skies.

ENVIRONMENTAL PROTECTION IN THE ATACAMA

Though it might appear devoid of any living creatures, the Atacama Desert is in fact a unique, precious and fragile ecosystem that supports an intricate web of life – from the South American grey fox, lava lizard and the viscacha (a relative of the chinchilla) to drought-tolerant plants like cacti, succulents and coneflowers and super-hardy strains of bacteria which might provide scientists with indications of the kinds of life-forms that could exist on other planets.

But as climate change takes hold, the balance that supports life in the desert is under threat. Simultaneously, the extraction of minerals – especially nitrates, copper, iodine and lithium (a key component in renewable battery technology) – is stripping salt-pans of moisture and threatening unique desert habitats.

The growth in tourism has had a major impact, too, especially in popular areas such as Los Flamencos National Reserve, the second-most visited in Chile, and home to the Atacama's main tourist hub, San Pedro de Atacama.

But the region is also pioneering new ways to manage tourism and industry in a more sustainable way. Since its foundation in 1990, the reserve has been co-managed by the Licken Antay, the indigenous people who have called the Atacama home for millennia. It's the first reserve in South America to trial this

WHEN TO GO

NOV-FEB
Peak season means major sights and attractions in the Atacama can be crowded, and prices higher.

SEP & OCT, MAR-MAY
Moderate temperatures make this the ideal time to visit.

JUN-AUG
Low season means cold weather and some places closed. Occasional rainfall can cause rare, spectacular desert blooms.

approach, and has demonstrated that it is entirely possible for national authorities and indigenous people to work together for the mutual benefit of all.

The partnership has also inspired the creation of community tourism initiatives and eco-tours, the best of which allow visitors to gain a deeper insight into the history, culture, craft and mythology of the Licken Antay people, and a window into the intimate affinity and understanding they share with their desert home.

Many local operators, companies, hotels and lodges have also committed to Chile's new sustainable travel standard, which rewards eco-friendly construction, reduced water use, waste treatment, thermal insulation, environmental protection and community involvement – a trend that will hopefully continue as tourism in the Atacama starts up again in 2022.

Above: the Atacama's Licken Antay people use coloured tassells to identify their llamas.

Left: hardy pink flamingos inhabit the Atacama's saline lagoons.

Previous spread: volcanic scenery in the Atacama.

08

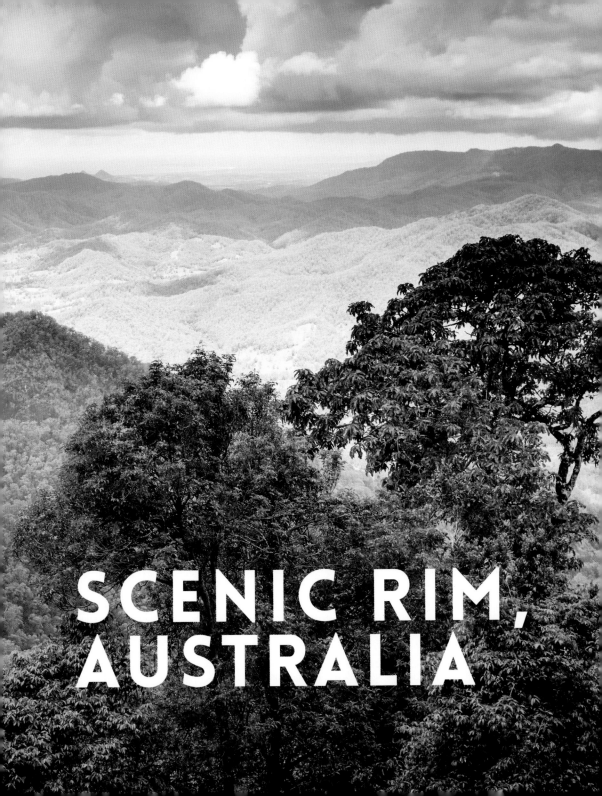

SCENIC RIM,
AUSTRALIA

UTC +10hr

Australian dollar

English, Aboriginal languages

Brisbane and Gold Coast international airports lie within an hour's drive of the Scenic Rim.

• *Secrets of the Scenic Rim* Robert Rankin
• *Binna Burra Begins* Don Marshall
• www.visitsenicrim. com.au

Between its ecolodges, wineries, six national parks and World Heritage-listed Gondwana Rainforests, the Scenic Rim has long had plenty going for it as a tourist destination. And after bouncing back from the Black Summer bushfires with a raft of new attractions – including Australia's newest Great Walk – and a renewed focus on sustainability, this lesser-known corner of Queensland is primed to become one of Australia's low-impact tourism power players.

OUT OF THE ASHES

Named for the verdant arc of mountains cradling a picturesque agricultural region in southeast Queensland, the Scenic Rim draws in-the-know bushwalkers and food lovers from around the world. Yet most people would be hard-pressed to pinpoint the region on a map. That was until September 2019, at least, when the region made global headlines after bushfires claimed Binna Burra Lodge, one of Australia's most iconic ecolodges, at the beginning of an unprecedented natural disaster that became known as the Black Summer. Then came Covid-19, which delayed the relaunch of local tourism until domestic travel restrictions began to ease. Despite this double blow, the Scenic Rim's recovery story is truly extraordinary.

On the one-year anniversary of the fires, Binna Burra Lodge, which is surrounded by Lamington National Park, reopened for business. After transforming its historic barn into a bushfire museum, the lodge is now planning to open Australia's first via ferrata – an exhilarating, gravity-defying climbing route with fixed chains and ladders – for 2022.

Also on the doorstep of Lamington National Park, O'Reilly's Rainforest Retreat recently transformed a basic campsite into a state-of-the-art camping destination, with safari tents and a communal hub providing spectacular views. And if you don't fancy toiling over a camp stove, order a Scenic Rim Farm Box from the same-name website, a gourmet hamper delivery service launched during the coronavirus outbreak to support farmers, packed with fresh seasonal produce (from quality meats to wine) and delivered with recipe ideas.

Arguably the region's most exciting post-bushfire tourism launch, however, is the Scenic Rim Trail. A guided luxury hike in Main Range National Park, which traces a lush, rainforest-covered ridgeline, the trail is linked by two purpose-built 'ecocamps'

Cool temperate rainforest in Lamington National Park.

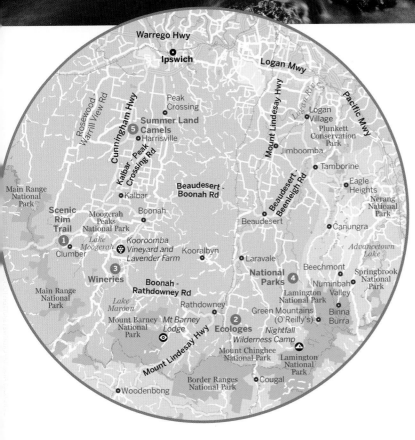

HIGHLIGHTS

1 **Scenic Rim Trail** Australia's newest Great Walk has redefined sustainable-luxe adventure.

2 **Ecolodges** Glamp at Nightfall Wilderness Camp or stay in a heritage cottage at Mt Barney Lodge.

3 **Wineries** 25 of them – and two breweries – call the region home.

4 **National parks** Bushwalk through the region's six superlative parks.

5 **Summer Land Camels** Buy camel cheese, vodka and skincare ranges from a sustainable farming outfit.

Jungle-swathed
Curtis Falls, just
one of the cascades
in the Scenic Rim's
Tamborine National
Park.

that take low-impact lodging to a new level. Spearheaded by boutique hotel group Spicers Retreats, it's the first trail in Queensland to form part of the Great Walks of Australia portfolio. But you can also experience the four-day walk on a budget, staying at public-access campsites managed by the Queensland National Parks and Wildlife Service.

A GREENER FUTURE

Sustainability has always been a dominant thread running through Scenic Rim tourism. And now the destination is further developing its commitment to environmental protection thanks to a partnership between Ecotourism Australia and WWF Australia which has seen the region, along with six other bushfire-affected areas around the country, receive support to achieve ECO Destination Certification in the coming years. Combining Ecotourism Australia's environmental criteria with the Green Destinations Standard for sustainable tourism, ECO Destination Certification will make it easier than ever for visitors to make planet-friendly travel choices.

Also rapidly greening up are the region's famous forests. After a whopping 36% of Queensland's Gondwana Rainforests was burned during the Black Summer fires, many feared for the worst. But this ancient ecosystem – home to species from which life on Earth evolved – is recovering faster than most locals expected. While some areas of Gondwana will bear scars for many years to come, the rebirth of the rainforest has added a new dimension to the tourism experience.

UNEXPECTED DELIGHTS

The Scenic Rim isn't just about rainforest adventures – first-time visitors might be surprised by the diversity of attractions to be found here. On the eastern fringe of the region, just 30 minutes from the heart of the Gold Coast, the misty slopes of Mount Tamborine town are packed with cafes, cellar doors and galleries; while just an hour from Brisbane, on the northern edge of the Scenic Rim, lies hatted (Australia's version of a Michelin star) restaurant Homage, which specialises in creative paddock-to-plate fare. In the heart of the region, you can sip on a craft beer in a heritage general-store-turned-brewery while tucking into the best Dutch-German bar food this side of Berlin. Stock up on lavender products (or wine) at nearby Kooroomba Vineyard and Lavender Farm before heading to Summer Land Camels, where the Persian camel-milk feta might just change your life.

Perfect for a long-weekend road trip, the Scenic Rim is dotted with epic landscapes and charming country towns offering a tasty slice of rural life, with cracking Queensland hospitality in plentiful supply too.

WHEN TO GO

JUN-AUG
Cool, dry mid-winter months see two major culinary festivals.

APR & MAY, SEP-NOV
Low rainfall and cooler temperatures make the autumn and spring months ideal for bushwalking.

DEC-MAR
High rainfall and hot, humid days make bushwalking challenging, though waterfalls are spectacular. The cooler climes of Mount Tamborine make it a popular escape from the summer heat.

> "The Scenic Rim isn't only home to incredible Gondwana rainforests, but also a bunch of friendly towns full of interesting country characters."
>
> LISA GROOM
> MANAGING DIRECTOR, PARK TOURS, AND GRANDDAUGHTER OF NATURALIST AND SCENIC RIM TOURISM PIONEER ARTHUR GROOM

185

0.9

VANCOUVER ISLAND, CANADÁ

GOOD TO KNOW

UTC -8hr

Canadian dollar

English

From the mainland, BC Ferries serves Swartz Bay (Victoria), Nanaimo and Comox. Victoria has a small international airport. Regional airlines serve Tofino, Campbell River and Port Hardy.

• *Vancouver Island Book of Everything* Peter Grant
• *Hard Knox: Musings from the Edge of Canada* Jack Knox
• *Popular Day Hikes: Vancouver Island* Theo Dombrowski

Move over Vancouver, it's time for Vancouver Island to have its moment in the spotlight. Once dismissed as a regional backwater where British Columbians went to retire, it's morphed into a cool hub of surfing beaches, boutique vineyards, community-led trail-building projects and locavore restaurants. If you're into riding Pacific breakers, getting from A to B by human-powered transport or frequenting a ski resort that isn't called Whistler, this could be your post-pandemic nirvana.

ISLAND LIFE

Easy-going, unsullied by excessive development and playing to a slower beat than mainland British Columbia, Vancouver Island is an ideal place to reset your compass after whatever the world throws at you. With a population of less than one million spread over a jagged landmass the size of Taiwan, the island has ample room for visitors to spread out and explore its forested mountains, storm-whipped beaches and calm, kayak-able inlets.

The south of the island, which dips below the 49th parallel, shelters Victoria, BC's low-rise capital, whose balmy climate is the mildest in Canada and whose pubs and tearooms recall an affectionate association with the UK.

Victoria launched Canada's oldest operating brewpub in 1984. Today, there are over 40 craft brewers on the island with new ventures gracing towns as small as Ucluelet (population 1717). The wine scene is equally buoyant. Striped vineyards colour the landscape of the fertile Cowichan Valley, the island's main agricultural region and base for a growing number of wine- and cider-makers – and even a tea farm.

Beyond Victoria, the culture is more ancient and diverse. Vancouver Island is home to 50 different First Nations groups, their indigenous stories ingrained in the fabric of land, from the emblematic totem poles of Duncan to the priceless artefacts in the U'mista Cultural Centre in Alert Bay.

And with a surfeit of big fauna, the island is like one big outdoor zoo. Black bears are common all over, whales breach in the waters around Victoria and Tofino and, unbeknownst to many, the island claims the densest population of cougars in North America.

ON YOUR BIKE

While Vancouver Island's road network isn't particularly extensive,

HIGHLIGHTS

1 **Tofino** Great beaches, sand surfing, wildlife and super Pacific sunsets.

2 **Victoria** Canadian-British cultural hub with tearooms, cricket ground, a castle and a superb museum.

3 **Cumberland** Excellent eating and drinking in a hip one-street village abutting top mountain-biking terrain.

4 **Alert Bay** First Nations treasure trove of art, museum pieces and the world's tallest totem pole.

5 **North Coast Trail** Boat-in access to long-distance wilderness hiking.

> "Vancouver Island's rugged ocean coastlines, lush rainforests, abundant wildlife and Indigenous culture are sought after by travellers and are at the root of our work to enhance sustainable travel."

ANTHONY EVERETT
PRESIDENT & CEO, TOURISM VANCOUVER ISLAND

its cycling paths are abundant and getting better by the year. Victoria is close to completing a 32km network of dedicated downtown bike lanes, while over on the west coast, C$51 million has been invested in a superb 25km-long bike path running between the surfing towns of Ucluelet and Tofino. Called ʔapsčiik ƚašii (pronounced 'ups-cheek ta-shee') in the local language, the trail closely tracks the coast through the Pacific Rim National Park and officially opens in 2022.

A SENSE OF COMMUNITY

As well as a destination for cyclists, Tofino is a classic example of a proud community-focused Vancouver Island town: small, handsome and vociferous in its support of local business over generic brands (no fast-food franchises here). Exposed to the full force of the Pacific, it is also Canada's surfing capital and, in recent years, has developed as a winter hub for storm-watching. Ringed by sea-stacks, islets and forested promontories, its beaches are sublime.

Over on the island's east coast, Qualicum Beach has followed a similar community-led path promoting everything from small-scale cheesemakers to restaurants plying

local products. Exemplifying its quirkiness are places like Free Spirit Spheres, an unconventional 'hotel' offering accommodation in three globe-shaped pods suspended in the forest.

Meanwhile, a wider community campaign is putting the finishing touches to a 770km-long multi-use trail running the full length of the island from Oak Bay to Cape Scott. Developing the so-called Vancouver Island Trail (VIT) has been a massive commitment undertaken mainly by

WHEN TO GO

JUN–AUG
Reliably warm and sunny with little rain.

APR & MAY, SEP & OCT
Variable weather and high chance of sporadic precipitation.

NOV–MAR
Highest rainfall, with snow and freezing conditions in the mountains and storms on the Pacific coast.

volunteers. Connecting existing paths along disused railway lines with newer sections over more rugged terrain, the task of knitting the route together began in 2009 and should be mostly complete by 2022.

The trail brushes past numerous island success stories. The Kinsol Trestle is a 100-year-old wooden railway bridge refurbished in 2011 after a concerted community campaign raised C$2 million to help restore it. Further north, in the Comox Valley, the former coal-mining town of

Cumberland reinvented itself in the 2010s as a hip mountain biking mecca thanks to a non-profit society that secured public trail access in a private forest. Close by, Mount Washington is the island's main ski area, a quieter, more budget-friendly alternative to world-famous Whistler.

After more than a year of lockdowns and restrictions, Vancouver Island is the perfect place to rediscover life's simple freedoms and revel in the spontaneity of life on Canada's wild west coast.

Above: keep your eyes trained on the coastal waters off Victoria and Tofino to see breaching humpback whales.

Left: Vancouver Island's Alert Bay is a treasure trove of First Nations culture.

Previous spread: surfing at Long Beach on the west coast of the island.

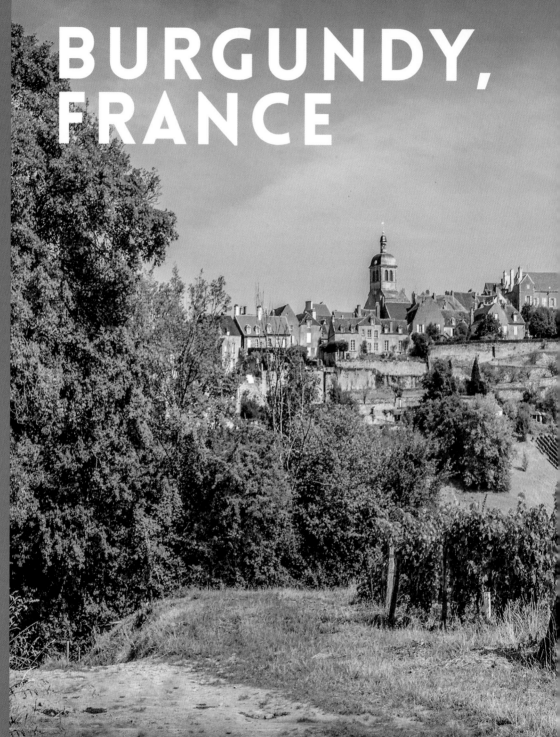

BURGUNDY, FRANCE

GOOD TO KNOW

UTC +1hr

Euro

French

By plane to Paris
Charles de Gaulle or
Orly airports, then
by car or train from
Paris Gare de Lyon to
main towns Dijon or
Beaune.

• *Puligny-Montrachet:
Journal of a Village
in Burgundy* Simon
Loftus
• *The Cook's Atelier:
Recipes, Techniques
and Stories from Our
French Cooking School*
Marjorie Taylor
and Kendall Smith
Franchini

From historic estates cradling fabled chateaux to emerald hills draped in vineyards venerated by passionate wine lovers the world over, the region of Burgundy (Bourgogne in French) is la belle France in one tantalising nutshell: fine food and wine, lyrical landscapes and unrivalled cultural heritage. In 2022 two blockbuster wine-tourism openings in this agricultural pocket of central-eastern France are a call to action to celebrate French vineyards and champion sustainable viticulture.

GRAND CRU COUNTRY

Ever since the Celts dabbled with vines, French *vin* (wine) has been more than a drink. It is a powerful reflection of the *terroir* (land), culture and history of its makers – which is precisely what makes slow touring around rural Burgundy's medieval villages, rustic family-run cellars, immaculate hand-groomed vines and sunflower-yellow mustard fields so enthralling.

Burgundy's epic vineyards extend approximately 250km from Chablis in the north almost to Beaujolais in the south. From perfumed Pinot Noirs to crisp Chablis with well-balanced minerality, this is where the world's most prized French wines have been honed to perfection by generations of *vignerons* (winemakers). The lifetime of unique know-how demanded by Burgundy's 84 Appellations d'Origine Contrôlée – winegrowing micro-regions with a unique combination of latitude, altitude, climate, sun exposure and soil – is gargantuan. World-renowned vintages pour out of Côte d'Or (literally 'Golden Hillside') – an oenophile nirvana marching up limestone, flint and clay hills in strict rows for about 60km south from dashing Burgundian capital Dijon. In the northern Côte d'Or, Côte de Nuits is Grand Cru country where some of France's smallest, most sought-after appellations are crafted. Touring the medieval vat house and presses, Cistercian cellar and original kitchens at 16th-century Château du Clos de Vougeot, followed by an indulgent *table d'hôte* tasting lunch with six different wines around a shared table in a private wing of the Renaissance chateau is a brilliant example of how Burgundian winemakers are working harder than ever to create immersive travel experiences that appeal to a smart new generation of wine enthusiasts.

A TALE OF SEVERAL CITIES

With such a colossal viticultural heritage, Burgundian winemakers are natural innovators. This is the region,

Dijon and its cathedral.

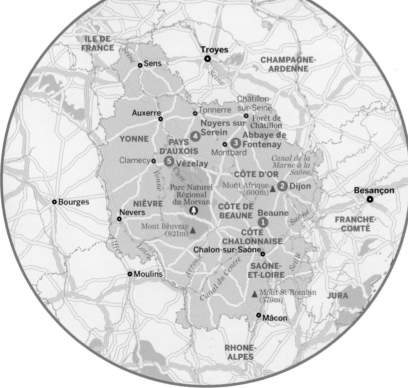

HIGHLIGHTS

1 Beaune Renowned vintages in the heart of vine-carpeted Côte d'Or.

2 Dijon Soak up artistic treasures curated by the dukes of Burgundy.

3 Abbaye de Fontenay Medieval monastic atmosphere at a serene Cistercian abbey.

4 Noyers-sur-Serein Lunch on hearty Burgundy cuisine in this medieval walled village.

5 Vézelay Basilica-crowned village of ancient cobblestone lanes surrounded by green hills.

As well as its viticultural draws, Burgundy boasts charming villages such as Unesco-listed Vézelay.

after all, where locals look at the soil rather than sky when discussing *climats* (the French word for a wine-growing plot or parcel of vines in Burgundy). Winemaking techniques have evolved rapidly to embrace widespread organic and biodynamic farming, and the region's current commitment to responsible viticulture is demonstrated by an explosive growth in environmentally certified vineyards – those officially certified as HEV (High Environmental Value), in recognition of excellent environmental practice, doubled in 2020 and continue to multiply. For visitors to the region, two landmark openings in 2022 shine a bright new green light on Burgundian wine culture.

First port of call: regional capital Dijon, heir to a glorious architectural heritage harking back to Gallo-Roman and Celtic antiquity. West of town, by the sweet spot where the bucolic Route des Grands Crus driving itinerary tangoes south into a glorious labyrinth of vineyards, a 13th-century orphanage-turned-hospital has been transformed into La Cité Internationale de la Gastronomie et du Vin (CIGV). A resolutely on-trend celebration of French gastronomy and wine, the striking €250 million complex includes a cooking school with live demos, wine school, restaurants, shops, exhibition space and labs.

Summer 2022 also raises the curtain on La Cité des Vins et des Climats de Bourgogne, with a green focus on sustainable winemaking and diversity in Burgundian terroir and tradition. Split across three celebrated wine towns, the flagship is in Beaune where some of the world's most expensive wines repose in cool cellars tucked beneath centuries-old streets. A spectacular Côte d'Or vineyard panorama crowns the contemporary, eco-sustainable building – a 24m-high tower resembling the corkscrew tendril of a vine. The permanent exhibition inside illuminates a wine heritage sufficiently precious to be a Unesco World Heritage treasure.

Seven Grands Crus grow on just 1 sq km of hillside in the picturesque town of Chablis. Contemporary vineyard gardens and ramped walkways at La Cité number two here, homed in a medieval cellar, will form a live exhibition on the seasonal rhythms of the wine-growing year, from winter-pruning bonfires to the autumnal grape harvest. Mâcon, on the banks of the River Saône, holds the third La Cité, in which visitors will be accompanied by a euphonic soundscape of melodies and calls of the wild. The multi-sensory activities – workshops, classes, tours, tastings and pairings – at all three sites promise French *joie de vivre* in buckets, not to mention an explorative journey into this esteemed wine region's *raison d'être*.

WHEN TO GO

JUN–AUG
Long, dry, sunny days encourage outdoor exploration.

APR & MAY, SEP & OCT
Late spring ushers in warm days; the grape harvest is an autumn highlight.

NOV–MAR
Winter is grey and chilly. Some hotels and restaurants close.

"Burgundy's new openings will highlight gastronomy and winegrowing – the essence of the region. They'll bring to light the professions and savoir-faire that create the region's unique identity."

LOÏC NIEPCERON
PRÉSIDENT, BOURGOGNE-FRANCHE-COMTÉ TOURISME

INDEX

MAKING BEST IN TRAVEL

Of all the amazing places and travel experiences on the planet, how do we choose the most exciting for the year ahead? It's a decision we do not take lightly. Read on for an overview of how the magic happens.

1 THE SURVEY

The annual *Best in Travel* survey is sent to the whole Lonely Planet family – every staff member, over 200 travel writers, bloggers, our publishing partners and more. In it we ask them to share their expertise on places and travel experiences that they predict will be buzzing in the year ahead.

2 THE TRAVEL HACK

In a typical year, we organise brainstorming events in Lonely Planet offices the world over, from Běijīng to Buenos Aires. This is when we come together to discuss the subject that inspires us the most: travel. Zoom calls were the substitute this year but the questions were the same. What are we excited about? Which destinations are doing something special? And where do we want to visit next – when we can travel once more?

3 SHORTLISTING

The results of the survey and Travel Hacks produce a longlist of more than a thousand ideas. This is then reviewed by Lonely Planet's *Best in Travel* team – an opinionated bunch of travel geeks with hundreds of thousands of travel miles between them. The team read every pitch and help whittle down the list to a shortlist of the very best places.

4 THE PANEL

The shortlist is then sent to a panel of travel experts: six people who live and breathe travel in their everyday lives. They scrutinise each idea and score them out of 100 for topicality, excitement and 'wow' factor. This year our panel included Roi Ariel, General Manager of the Global Sustainable Tourism Council; Uwern Jong, Editor-in-Chief of *OutThere*; Tharik Hussain, an Islamic travel expert; Sarah Greaves-Gabbadon, an expert on Caribbean travel; Martin Heng, an Accessible Travel advocate; and Melanie Lieberman, a Senior Editor at www.thepointsguy.com.

5 THE FINAL LIST

When the panel results are in, the list is finalised and shared with a trusted handful of people at Lonely Planet until October when, finally, the selection of the best places and travel experiences for the year ahead is shared with the world.

CONTRIBUTORS

ALEX CREVAR
A travel writer for 20 years, Alex Crevar's stories combine culture and adventure. Follow him on Instagram, @alexcrevar, and visit www.alexcrevar.com.

ALI WUNDERMAN
Ali Wunderman is a freelance travel and wildlife journalist with work in *The Washington Post*, *Condé Nast Traveler*, *Travel + Leisure* and *Forbes*. Ali lives between Montana and Belize, and you can follow her travels via Instagram at @aliwunderman.

ANDREA SCHULTE-PEEVERS
Born and raised in Germany and educated in London and Los Angeles, Andrea Schulte-Peevers has visited some 80 countries. She has earned her living as a professional travel writer for over two decades and has authored over 100 books for Lonely Planet, including all editions of the guides to Germany and Berlin. Follow her at @aschultepeevers.

ANTHONY HAM
Anthony (www.anthonyham. com) has written more than 140 guidebooks for Lonely Planet, covering Africa, Australia, Brazil, Spain and the US. He is the author of *The Last Lions of Africa*, and can be followed at @AnthonyHamWrite (Twitter) or @anthonyham2002 (Instagram).

BRENDAN SAINSBURY
Brendan Sainsbury is based in British Columbia, Canada. He has travelled to 75 countries and contributed to 60 Lonely Planet guidebooks covering everywhere from Alaska to Mozambique. Follow him on Twitter @sainsburyb.

BRETT ATKINSON
Brett Atkinson writes about travel from his home in Auckland, and has contributed to many Lonely Planet guidebooks. Follow him @travelwriternz on Instagram and Twitter, and find him online at www.brett-atkinson.net.

CLIFTON WILKINSON
Clifton has worked in travel publishing for over 20 years, writing and editing books, articles and reviews, as well as being Lonely Planet's Iceland and UK editor.

CRAIG MCLACHLAN
An itinerant Kiwi, Craig has been writing about Japan and other destinations for Lonely Planet since the late 1990s. Check out www.craigmclachlan.com.

EMILY MATCHAR
Emily Matchar lives in Hong Kong, though she visits her native North Carolina as much as possible. She writes for magazines and newspapers and has contributed to many Lonely Planet titles.

HARMONY DIFO
Harmony Difo is a lifestyle, culture and travel journalist creating short and long-form content across all formats and continents. Her website is www.harmonydifo.com.

JAMES BAINBRIDGE
James is a Cape Town-based writer in whose work has appeared in publications from *BBC Travel* to *Condé Nast Traveller*. You can read James's travel articles at www.jamesbainbridge.net

JESSICA LEE
Jessica Lee is a travel writer specialising in the Middle East and North Africa. She's co-authored multiple editions of Lonely Planet guidebooks and her work has appeared in *BBC Travel*, *Wanderlust Magazine*, *Afar*, *CNN Travel*, *The Telegraph*, *The Independent* and *British Airways High Life Magazine*. She tweets @jessofarabia.

JOE BINDLOSS
Joe Bindloss has been writing about travel for Lonely Planet and other publishers for more than 20 years, focusing on the Indian Subcontinent and Southeast Asia. He has worked on more than 60 Lonely Planet guidebooks and he writes regularly for the *Guardian*, *Telegraph* and other newspapers. Follow Joe at @joe_planet.

JOHN HECHT
Mexico-based John Hecht has contributed to more than 20 Lonely Planet guidebooks and trade publications. He has spent considerable time in Mérida as a co-author on several editions of *Cancún, Cozumel & the Yucatán.*

MELANIE LIEBERMAN
Melanie Lieberman is currently a senior travel editor at The Points Guy. Prior to TPG, Melanie was an editor at *Travel + Leisure* magazine, and her work has appeared in *Bloomberg Pursuits,* Yahoo Travel, *Jetsetter, Boston Common* magazine, LUXE City Guides and *Saveur* magazine, among others. She has been featured as a travel expert on television, radio, podcasts and in print, and she has been recognized for her poetry, prose and playwriting in various competitions and festivals.

NICOLA WILLIAMS
Border-hopping is a way of life for British writer Nicola Williams, who lives on the southern side of Lake Geneva. She has authored some 100 guidebooks and inspirational reference titles for Lonely Planet and can be tracked on the road at @tripalong (Instagram and Twitter).

NOO SARO-WIWA
Noo Saro-Wiwa is the author of *Looking for Transwonderland: Travels in Nigeria* (Sunday Times Travel Book of the Year, 2012).

ODA O'CARROLL
Haiing from the midwest of Ireland, Oda scratches her travel itch authoring titles for Lonely Planet. She also writes for *The Irish Times, The Guardian,* BBC, *Cara* and *Tatler* magazines and in 2012 founded a children's travel website.

OLIVER BERRY
Oliver Berry is a writer and photographer based in Cornwall. He has travelled to 69 countries and six continents. You can read his latest work at www.oliverberry.com.

PETER DRAGICEVICH
In a publishing career spanning 30 years, Peter has written for a wide variety of newspapers and magazines – both in his native Aotearoa/ New Zealand and abroad – and has co-authored over 60 different titles for Lonely Planet.

PHILLIP TANG
Phillip Tang writes about travel and his two loves, Asia and Latin America, for Lonely Planet. More at www.hellophillip.com and Instagram @mrtangtangtang.

PIERA CHEN
Piera is a travel writer based in Taipei, but scattered over North America, China and various exotic destinations, real or imagined. She believes that if writing is the most disembodied of the arts, travel writing and poetry are the genres that make it less so, and this is why she's in love with both. Instagram, Twitter, Facebook: @pierachen.

SARAH REID
Sarah Reid is a multi-award-winning Australian travel writer and editor with a passion for sustainable adventure travel. She contributes to a number of top travel titles including Adventure.com, *BBC Travel, National Geographic Travel, Qantas* magazine, *Travel + Leisure* and more. She is also the author of Lonely Planet's *The Sustainable Handbook,* amongst other titles. Follow her on Instagram @ecotravelist.

STEPHEN LIOY
Stephen Lioy is a photographer, writer and hiker based in Central Asia. A 'once in a lifetime' Eurotrip and subsequent move to China set the stage for a semi-nomadic lifestyle based on sharing his experiences with would-be travellers. Follow Stephen's travels at www.asia-hikes.com or see his photography at www.stephenlioy.com.

THARIK HUSSAIN
Tharik is an author specialising in Islamic culture and heritage. His new book *Minarets in the Mountains: A Journey into Muslim Europe,* is the first by a Muslim travel writer to explore indigenous Muslim Europe. Follow him on twitter: @_tharikhussain, instagram: @tharik_hussain or facebook.com/TharikHussainAuthor.

Best in Travel 2022

October 2021

Published by Lonely Planet Global Limited

ABN 36 005 607 983

www.lonelyplanet.com

1 2 3 4 5 6 7 8 9 10

General Manager, Publishing Piers Pickard
Associate Publisher Robin Barton
Editors Cliff Wilkinson, Polly Thomas
Art Director Kristina Juodenas
Layout Designer Jo Dovey
Print Production Nigel Longuet

Written by: Alex Crevar (Slovenia); Ali Wunderman
(Belize); Andrea Schulte-Peevers (Freiburg); Anthony
Ham (Mauritius); Brendan Sainsbury (Puerto Rico,
Vancouver Island); Brett Atkinson (Cook Islands); Clifton
Wilkinson (Kent, Westfjords); Craig McLachlan (Shikoku);
Emily Matchar (Anguilla); Harmony Difo (Atlanta); James
Bainbridge (Malawi); Jessica Lee (Egypt); Joe Bindloss
(Nepal); John Hecht (Mérida); Melanie Lieberman (West
Virginia); Nicola Williams (Burgundy, Florence); Noo
Saro-Wiwa (Lagos); Oda O'Carroll (Dublin); Oliver Berry
(Norway, Atacama Desert); Peter Dragicevich (Auckland);
Phillip Tang (Gyeongju); Piera Chen (Taipei); Sarah Reid
(Scenic Rim); Stephen Lioy (Xingshuabanna); Tharik
Hussain (Oman); Tom Hall (Introduction)

Printed in Singapore

ISBN 9781788689199

© Lonely Planet 2021

© photographers as indicated 2021

Lonely Planet Global Limited

Digital Depot, Roe Lane (off Thomas St),
Digital Hub, Dublin 8, D08 TCV4 Ireland

STAY IN TOUCH
lonelyplanet.com/contact